BLUE JEANS
IN
HIGH PLACES

THE COMING MAKEOVER
OF AMERICAN POLITICS

MIKE McCABE

LITTLE CREEK PRESS®
A DIVISION OF KRISTIN MITCHELL DESIGN, LLC

Mineral Point, Wisconsin USA

Little Creek Press®
A Division of Kristin Mitchell Design, Inc.
5341 Sunny Ridge Road
Mineral Point, Wisconsin 53565

Book Design and Project Coordination:
Little Creek Press

Second Printing
January 2015

Printed in Wisconsin, United States of America

For more information or to order books,
please visit: www.littlecreekpress.com

Library of Congress Control Number: 2014946311

ISBN-10: 0989978400
ISBN-13: 978-0-9899784-0-8

Dedicated to the hungry hearts of true citizens.

This book never would have been written absent the love, support and encouragement of my wife, Marilyn Feil, and my son, Casey McCabe. This is theirs as much as it is mine.

I also owe a large debt of gratitude to Kristin Mitchell for believing in this book, and to my editor Carl Stratman for his careful attention to detail and many excellent suggestions for improvements. A special thank you goes to Dave and Diane Pauly for their astounding generosity of spirit in helping me on my way, to Lori Compas for her unique blend of infectious enthusiasm and constructive criticism, to Mike Moskoff for his steady encouragement, and to hundreds of others who urged me on both emotionally and financially with their generous responses to the publisher's appeal for crowdfunding. Their faith that the book would be worth reading without seeing a word I'd written was as inspiring as it is heartwarming.

INTRODUCTION

American politics is caught in a time warp. If other aspects of our lives mirrored the way we think and talk about politics and act as citizens, we would all still be wearing knickers or petticoats, dancing the Charleston and telegraphing messages to each other in Morse code.

Life in America bears little resemblance to life at the nation's founding, or even the America our great-grandparents knew. The roofs over our heads, the food on our tables, the clothes on our backs—all have changed dramatically. The way we work, how we travel, and what we do with our leisure time are completely different and growing more so by the day. But much about civic life has evolved barely at all, as if frozen in time.

New slang enters our language almost daily and is quickly incorporated into conversation at work or school or social gatherings, yet our political vocabulary has remained remarkably static. New businesses are regularly being started, bombarding us with new goods and services catering to our ever-changing tastes, while old products are continuously reformulated and repackaged to account for evolving appetites. American political parties and their trademarks, on the other hand, have stayed constant for ages. We have little choice but to perpetually upgrade our workplace skills to keep pace with the demands of a fast-moving global economy, but both the demands and opportunities of citizenship are largely unchanged.

Democracy is a living thing, and in America it is in a state of suspended animation.

No wonder so many people feel disillusioned about politics and detached from the democratic process. The more the world changes and the more politics stays the same, the greater the cause for alienation. Inside-the-beltway pundits endlessly write and talk about the doings and failings of government and the whims and inclinations of voters, but with diminishing effect. American politics is growing increasingly disconnected from American life.

This is not the first time in our nation's history that politics has fallen out of step with the times. If history is any guide, the innovators who will help us think our way out of our current trap will come from unexpected locations.

In the fashion world, trends are set in places like Paris, New York and London. In film, all eyes are on Hollywood. In business, western centers of commerce still may set the tone but much of the action is increasingly found in Hong Kong, Dubai, Beijing, Singapore and Shanghai. When invention comes to American politics, it only makes sense to assume its origins would be Washington. But history indicates otherwise. Past political trend-setting has come from nowhere near the Potomac River. When American politics twice before underwent extensive remodeling, it did not happen in the nation's capital. Curiously enough, the renovation was engineered in my home state of Wisconsin, of all places.

As political systems go, America's is comparatively young. But our democracy looks old and sickly at the moment. Politics in our country has again become outdated and needs a totally new look. Recollection of past facelifts inspires much of what you will find in the following pages. Indications of trends in the making and imagination of enterprising citizenship not yet pondered inspire the rest.

CHAPTER 1

CLUES FROM
CLARK COUNTY

Wisconsin's Clark County is where I did most of my growing up. I moved there with my family in 1971 shortly before my eleventh birthday. My dad was north of 50 but was finally realizing his lifelong dream of getting back to farming full time. His family lost their farm during the Great Depression. My mom—a city kid—lost her father. Jobless and emotionally tortured by the daily reminders of his inability to provide for his family, he went off on his own, leaving his wife, two sons and two daughters to fend for themselves.

After fighting in World War II, my dad returned to get on with his life, met my mom and the two were married. For years, they made their way by farming on halves, the northern equivalent of sharecropping. They were tenant laborers, working the land and tending the dairy herd while splitting their earnings with the landowner.

While starting a family—enduring a still birth before the arrival of three healthy daughters—they toiled for southern Wisconsin landlords, first on a farm in the Whitewater area and then on another near Beloit. By the time my brother was born, mom and dad had saved up enough for a down payment on a farm of their own. A few miles outside the Rock County community of Evansville, it was not much more than a hobby farm, a mere 80 acres capable of supporting the smallest of cattle herds. Dad worked full-time in a factory in town, and in his spare time milked our three cows, planted and harvested the crops and kept the machinery in working order. Mom, my sisters, my brother and I did our part too, helping with the barn chores and taking care of a small flock of chickens and a few pigs. It was there I spent the first 10 years of my life.

My parents scrimped and saved and eventually pulled together enough money to buy a full-size, family-supporting dairy farm (with the help of a sizeable bank loan, of course). We moved a couple of hundred miles north where land prices were cheaper, and landed in Clark County.

Situated about halfway between the cities of Wausau and Eau Claire, near a tiny dot on the map named Curtiss, our new home was a standard Wisconsin family dairy farm—200 acres and 40 cows. I'd never seen my dad happier. It had taken him close to 40 years, but he had made it all the way back to what his family had before the Depression hit.

Clark County was the epicenter of the dairy industry in the state known as "America's Dairyland." Still is to this day. It had more cows than people. Still does. The most recent census put the entire human population in the county at a shade under 35,000[1]—a whopping 29 people per square mile. According to U.S. Department of Agriculture figures, Clark County boasts 67,000 cows, the most anywhere in the state.[2]

To know Clark County, first know that I never thought of our family as poor. Like most farm kids, we wore hand-me-down clothes. We had no health insurance. One time, when my brother had finished filling a cart with cow feed, he threw the pitchfork he was using on top of the loaded cart before noticing that I had grabbed the cart to wheel it away. The fork went straight through my hand. I wasn't taken to the doctor. Mom wrapped my hand with a poultice of Epsom salts and hoped for the best. Another time my right leg had an unfortunate encounter with a barbed wire fence and the fence won. Ripped a series of gashes from my thigh to my calf. There was no trip to the doctor to get stitched up. Just more Epsom salts. My first visit to a dentist's office was at the age of 22, after I'd left the farm. My family let my teeth decay and grow crooked, concentrating instead on keeping my soul straight.

Still, I had reasons not to feel poor. We never went hungry out there on the farm and were considerably better off than most of our neighbors.

Clark County is one of the five poorest counties in Wisconsin,[3] a state in the bottom half nationally in per capita income.[4] The county could not have been comparing any more favorably when I lived there. As I finished up high school in the late 1970s, I was watching bankers foreclose on neighbor after neighbor, throwing them off their land and taking away both their livelihood and their way of life.

By 1984, Hollywood caught wind of the crisis in rural America. Three movies depicting the plight of family farmers—*Country*, *Places in the Heart* and *The River*—shared the big screen that year. The music industry also noticed something was wrong in farm country. The first Farm Aid concert was performed in 1985.[5] Their art mirrored our reality. Families like mine lived those films and those songs.

To understand Clark County's essential character as I knew it then, let me tell you about Les Sturz. Neighbors had many a good laugh at Les's expense, sniggering about how he "wasn't the sharpest tool in the shed" or was "a few bricks short of a load." Some insisted he was illiterate, but I saw and heard enough to believe he could read and write despite his apparent lack of much formal education. He spoke with what I can only describe as a strong Northwoods drawl. Vowels were stretched and words starting with the "th" sound became "dis," "dat," "dem" and "doze." Words ending with that unpronounceable sound came out as "wit" and "boat." His remarks were generously sprinkled with "you betcha" and "dontcha know," and most every sentence was punctuated with "eh!" You or I might say, "Please join me." From Les, it was, "Come wit, eh?" It took some getting used to, but it wasn't hard to follow what he was saying. His way of talking fit him, along with the buzz cut, the threadbare flannel shirts and the shit-kicker work boots. Les was hard to dislike. He was as good-natured as he was strong-backed and hard-working.

Compared to the Sturz family, mine was very well off. Decisions like foregoing health insurance and eating Velveeta instead of the cheese our milk went to make kept our farm profitable. Les's family wasn't so lucky. Shortly after the bank issued a notice of foreclosure, his father was found hanging from a rafter in a shed.

His dad took his own life at harvest time. The rains wouldn't stop that year, leaving the fields so muddy it was next to impossible to harvest the crops. One day we had a tractor hopelessly buried in a corn field, up to its axles in mud. We tried pulling it out with another tractor and got that one stuck too. The next thing we see is Les Sturz on his family's bright orange Allis Chalmers tractor racing down the road to our rescue. He fastened a chain from his tractor to ours, pulled us out of our rut, and proceeded to pull us around the field the rest of that day until our corn was harvested. Of course we returned the favor on his farm in the days to come, but that still didn't strike me as a fair exchange considering the circumstances. The sight of him coming down the road that day to help a neighbor in need—just days after his father committed suicide and just months before the Sturz family had their farm taken from them—is forever burned in my memory.

Les Sturz was not a worldly man in the well-traveled sense. He was not politically savvy, or even politically aware. For what little time he spent in school, he was surely not much of a student. But he was a good teacher. He gave me some of my first and most important lessons about the meaning of the common good. Les didn't know much, but he knew of the value of thinking *we first* instead of *me first*.

As I finished high school, I could read the handwriting on the wall. The future looked bleak for small family farms. So I headed off to college.

Living in Madison all these years later, I regularly encounter people who marvel at what they consider the stupidity of people like my old neighbors who vote against their own self interest. How can they possibly believe the Republicans' feed-the-rich policies will benefit them? How can some of the poorest people cast their political lot with the 1%? To them, the good folks of Clark County are an indecipherable riddle.

Some years ago, Tom Frank wrote the book *What's the Matter with Kansas?* The story chronicled the transformation of a hotbed of progressive politics into a mainstay of turn-back-the-clock conservatism. He could just as well have been writing about Clark County.

Two generations ago, Clark County was represented by a fiery populist, Frank Nikolay. No truer progressive ever served in Wisconsin's legislature. A generation ago, around the time my family moved into the area, the county was sending Tom Harnisch to the State Capitol. Harnisch was a more moderate Democrat than Nikolay but a Democrat all the same. Clark County went on to be represented in recent times by the likes of Scott Suder, a rabid right winger and Tea Party Republican[6] who rose to the position of majority leader in the state Assembly.

Liberals dwell on how Republicans used social issues like abortion, gay marriage and gun rights as wedges to splinter off low-income rural voters who used to vote for Democrats and now reliably support Republicans. The left overlooks the economic wedge the right skillfully exploited.

No Hollywood producer ever told the Sturz family's story. No musicians played a benefit concert for them. No union negotiated on their behalf or stood in solidarity with Les and his widowed mother as they were made to leave their home.

Now, don't get me wrong. I believe in labor unions. Joining a union in the workplace is a basic human right. That's not just me talking, it is a statement found in Article 23 of the *Universal Declaration of Human Rights*,[7] approved by the United Nations General Assembly on December 10, 1948 with the United States voting yes.

The biggest problem with unions is they don't represent and protect *enough* working people. Belonging to a union may be a right, but for most workers it is not a practical option. Today, America's working class is divided and conquered. When everyone from factory workers and migrant laborers to postal workers and police officers were unionized, they were a potent force in the national economy and the nation's politics. But when unionization started slipping seriously in the private sector in the latter part of the twentieth century, the public sector was left as the last bastion of true union brawn. And that started alienating some groups of working people from others.

Non-union workers like farmers who were being driven from their land and factory workers who were being downsized and outsourced and offshored to death started to feel growing resentment toward better-off unionized government employees who held on to pension plans, employer-paid insurance and other benefits that were long gone in the private sector.

This created an opening for Republicans to build a rich-poor alliance... and a governing majority in Wisconsin. Republicans asked people in places like Clark County if they had pensions, and the answer was invariably no. Well, your taxes pay for the public workers' pensions, they'd tell them. Do you have health insurance? No. So how do you feel about paying for theirs? Are you getting pay raises? No. Well, they are... at your expense! It's not that the Republicans offered people any realistic hope of getting any of these things; they just very effectively played on very real slights to fan the flames of envy.

My dad had an eighth grade education. In his view of the political world, as he told me more times than I can count, the Democrats were the party of the poor and the Republicans were the party of the rich. If he were alive today, he would not be able to make heads or tails of the Tea Party movement. He would be confounded by the fact that some of the poorest Americans are among the Republican Party's most faithful supporters. In the 2010 election for governor in Wisconsin, Republican standard bearer Scott Walker carried eight of the 10 counties with the lowest per capita income. He lost in Menominee County, which is made up entirely of an Indian reservation and where only 752 votes were cast. And he narrowly lost Crawford County. But overall Walker won by 13 percentage points, with a vote margin of 8,400 out of just over 66,500 votes in Wisconsin's 10 poorest counties.[8]

In Clark County, one of the state's five poorest, Walker got 61% of the vote. In early 2011, Walker and his allies in the state legislature proceeded to strip most public workers of their ability to unionize and the right to collectively bargain with their employer. The action prompted mass demonstrations. Crowds on the Capitol grounds swelled to more than 100,000 protesters. Eventually they took their protest to the streets, gathering close to a million petition signatures to force a recall election. With the help of millionaires and billionaires from one coast of the United States to the other,[9] Walker raised and spent more than $36 million and had tens of millions more spent on his behalf by supportive business interests to survive the attempt in 2012 to remove him from office two years before his term was due to expire.[10] He carried Clark County by more than 30 percentage points.[11]

Walker's popularity in Clark County, when he has done next to nothing to visibly benefit the area, says much more about his opponents' weaknesses than his own strengths. And rural Wisconsin serves as an illustrative microcosm in this regard.

Democrats have broken the political law of universality. They may say we're all in this together and need to look out for each other, but people in places like rural Clark County don't see Democrats practicing what they preach. When the Democrats won the hearts of a majority of people in the past, it was because the party had a big hand in creating things that tangibly benefited everyone or at least directly touched every American family in a major way. Social Security and Medicare. Rural electrification. The GI Bill. The interstate highway system.

Two generations ago, when Clark County supported Frank Nikolay, the actions of Democrats were helping all of working-class America. Strong private *and* public sector unions were the financial backbone of the party. A generation ago, when Tom Harnisch was representing the county in the legislature, the private sector unions were losing steam and the Democrats were becoming increasingly reliant on the government workers and their unions for political backing. Their policies reflected that.

As the heady days of the New Deal and Great Society receded in the rear view mirror, Democrats grew steadily less able to deliver better health or retirement security or higher pay to all. Government workers who were among the last to enjoy strong union representation benefited from the Democrats' toil, but not many others. What is the modern equivalent of the GI Bill that offers every family a path to vocational training or an affordable college education? Where is the digital age's equivalent of rural electrification or the interstate highway system?

People in Clark County are not stupid. They noticed that the Democrats did not have good answers to these questions.

Most people across rural Wisconsin and throughout rural America see Democrats working for health and retirement security and better pay for government workers, but not for them. They see that the bankers who took away their land have two parties working for them, but can't see one that is on their side.

In places like Clark County, the Democratic Party is seen as the party of government, and most people hate the government. Why? Because increasingly they see it as corrupt, run by self-serving people they view as crooked. They don't believe government is working for them, and if it's not going to work for them, then they'd prefer to keep it as small as possible. The Republican Party is seen as the anti-government party, and has become the default option in Clark County. My old stomping grounds are hardly alone in that regard.

The party of the poor no longer has the poorest in our society with them. The unions that supplied them with a power base have been under siege, first in the private sector and now in the public. With union power dwindling, and union money drying up, Democrats now get far more of their campaign money from business interests than from labor unions.[12] The combination of their reliance on the 1% for donations and their allegiance to what little is left of the unions is alienating them from the poor in places like Clark County. It's hard to imagine Democrats ever winning in Wisconsin's rich counties like Ozaukee, Waukesha and Washington. All of which leaves the Democrats between a rock and a hard place.

It shows. A young woman who was born and raised in farm country went away to school before returning home some years later to launch a bid for a seat in the state Assembly. She told me that operatives in state Democratic headquarters lectured her that the key to winning was to avoid being pinned down on any issue. The Democrats' nominee for governor gave her the same advice, recommending that she remain as vague as possible in answering any policy questions and telling her—to her face—to just be "present and pleasant." She did as she was told. She lost.

You lose in politics sometimes. But when you lose, you need to lose with a purpose. Something has to be gained from every defeat. Seeds planted during today's loss grow into the fruits of tomorrow's win. Present and pleasant serves no purpose.

In victory there is still vulnerability for the Republicans in places like Clark County. Today's GOP seems utterly uninterested in lifting a finger to create greater economic and health and retirement security for working families. Republican politicians in Wisconsin have no discernible rural agenda. They harvest votes in farm country, but their actions do nothing to create better harvests there.

In defeat there is still opportunity for the Democrats. Liberal positions favoring reproductive freedom, gay rights and gun control measures like criminal background checks as a condition for firearm purchases will keep them in good stead with left-of-center voters. And catering to the last remaining cash constituency loyal to the Democrats alone—the public employee unions—will enable them to keep rolling up large vote totals in Madison and other locales where government is a major component of the economy. But in Wisconsin, winning in Milwaukee and Madison and a few other liberal enclaves does not a majority party make. Continuing to ignore the law of universality and failing to breed new Frank Nikolays is no formula for electoral success statewide.

Farm country used to be fertile territory for Democrats, but they have been getting their heads handed to them in rural Wisconsin for quite some time now, including in almost all of the state's poorest counties. It's hard to be the party of the rural poor when you don't have a rural agenda. Name me a signature modern-day Democratic program or policy addressing the challenges facing rural communities. It's not that the Democrats don't have a compelling or even coherent rural agenda. They don't have a rural agenda, period.

Neither major party truly cares about Clark County. One neglects its residents but takes their votes for granted while the other offers up little more than condescension and has written it off. Neither has anything resembling a true rural agenda. There is a reason for that. Of the roughly 900 zip codes in Wisconsin, most of the political money comes from barely 30 of them.[13] Every one of those "giving zips" is either urban or suburban. The major parties don't talk about rural problems because they can't raise any money with such talk. Rural people aren't big campaign donors. A great many Americans have much in common with rural Wisconsinites. Coming out of the Great Recession, one in three Americans found themselves either living in poverty or that perilous place just above the official poverty line.[14] Poor people don't make political donations either, which explains why no new war on poverty was launched when poverty rose to historic proportions and why even those politicians belonging to what my dad saw as the party of the poor take such pains to confine their expressions of concern to the plight of the middle class and working families. Nor are they talking much anymore about the gender pay gap, despite the fact that women still make less than 80 cents for every dollar men earn.[15] Well, when it comes to political giving, women give about a quarter for every dollar men contribute.[16]

For rural folk, or the urban poor or women or racial minorities or any number of other demographic groups in America, there are two problems in American politics that surpass any other. The first is that most Americans no longer believe they are being represented in Washington or in state capitals like Madison, their voices are no longer being heard and their interests are not being served. The second problem is that most Americans are correct. They have good reason to feel that way.

There is a cancer growing in the body of democracy. Most politicians in both major parties have been slow to come to terms with the severity of the disease and the impact it is having on their standing with the public.

Which brings me back to Les Sturz. The spirit of neighbor helping neighbor that he personified is nowhere to be seen on today's political landscape. Some will say that nostalgia is all that's left of this ethic. It's true that Americans don't trust each other like we used to.[17] And it's unquestionably true that the ties that bind us together have frayed. The best-known analysis of why this might be comes from author Robert Putnam's *Bowling Alone*, which chronicled two decades' worth of decline in what he called America's "social capital."

But social capital won't be remanufactured by going bowling. Or by joining clubs. Or by connecting on social networks. We need to prosper together. We need to make key decisions about how our society functions together. Today, Clark County is full of people who've never known the brotherhood of a union. They've grown full of resentment for having to pay for others to have things they don't have themselves. Their concerns do not come up when lawmakers talk with each other or with the lobbyists in the marble corridors in Washington or Madison; their issues aren't fodder for floor speeches in what passes for debates in those ornate legislative chambers; their problems do not get fixed there. While waiting for authentic representation, they have joined with their rural brethren to form one half of the Republicans' rich-poor governing coalition in Wisconsin, in Kansas, and all across the country. That the governing made possible by this coalition is done for the benefit of the rich is beyond dispute.[18] Income and wealth inequality in America is real, it is growing, and it is the natural byproduct of conscious political decisions and government policies.[19]

Wittingly or not, Clark County has done its part to keep the architects of these policies in power. Despite an abysmal job-creation record,[20] a cloud of scandal and criminal investigations[21] and nearly a million angry citizens petitioning for his removal, Scott Walker grew more popular in Clark County in 2012 and his rich-poor alliance worked wonders for him. The Democrats proved unable to beat Wisconsin's most polarizing political figure since Joe McCarthy,[22] one bankrolled by millionaires and billionaires, some of whom could vote in the election and most of whom could not.[23]

Wisconsin Democrats were positively flummoxed by the fact that the majority of voters could not be persuaded to find their party's standard bearer—Milwaukee's affable mayor Tom Barrett—preferable to Walker. Finger pointing ensued. Some blamed President Obama for not coming to Wisconsin to stump for Barrett. Some blamed the populist former Senator Russ Feingold for not volunteering to run in Barrett's place. Others fumed about the folly of the unions spending $4.5 million in a failed attempt to secure the Democratic nomination for their favored candidate—Dane County liberal Kathleen Falk, who obligingly pledged to veto any future state budget that did not restore public employee bargaining rights. That promise impressed union leaders, but not voters. She lost badly in the Democratic primary.

Monday morning quarterbacks even blamed the citizenry itself, calling the petition drive to force a recall election a strategic blunder. Party insiders wouldn't go there, but in what former party chair Joe Wineke described as a "circular firing squad," Democratic stalwarts aimed shots at everyone from the DNC to Wineke's successor as

MIKE McCABE

state party chair, Mike Tate. For his part and presumably his party's, Tate said there were no regrets, gamely insisting "some things are worth losing over."

The scapegoating raged for weeks and even months, but the recall election post-mortems never did come around to the question of whether the Democratic Party could deal with, or even recognize, how damaged its brand really is. Democrats remained baffled, continuing to see all those Walker voters as an indecipherable riddle. In Clark County, in this place with more cows than people, there are important clues to the riddle. To most eyes, in Clark County anyway, the Democratic Party is the party of government and government employees and their unions. Most people hate the government. How do you build a governing majority with a brand people hate?

You don't.

CHAPTER 2
A DREAM DOWNSIZED

America is up to its eyeballs in problems. Family farmers that once formed the spine of vibrant rural communities in Clark County are an endangered species, and the small-town life in such places is withering away. But there is equally disturbing inner-city decay and despair in once-gleaming urban centers. Detroit is a bankrupt shadow of its former self. New Orleans struggles to bounce back from the devastation of a bygone natural disaster. From Los Angeles on one coast to New York on the other, there are drug-infested, violence-riddled neighborhoods where hope is hard to find. There are overflowing prisons and overwhelmed schools. In suburbia, financial insecurities are as endemic as the homes and business establishments are generic. And then in the escapist gated communities, birds of a gilded feather flock together in hopes that others' struggles can remain out of mind if they are kept out of sight.

Behind those gates might be the only place where the anxiety shared by most Americans cannot be found. Rural Americans know the angst of which I speak. Urban and suburban dwellers surely know it. So do blacks. And whites. Americans of every other color too. Men. Women. And especially our nation's youth.

I am talking about the one thing that is more responsible than any other for the current dismal state of affairs in American government, as well as the coming political upheaval. I am talking about the downsizing of the American Dream. I am talking about the loss of faith in that most American of assumptions, namely that the next generation's reach will exceed the previous generation's grasp.

It has dawned on most everyone that for the first time in our nation's history, we have a generation of parents who no longer can find enough reason to believe their children will be better off than they are. That article of faith always has been at the core of the American Dream. The core has rotted.

On the cover of the December 2011 edition of *Foreign Affairs,* the magazine asked "Is America Over?"[1] The question was posed in reference to America's status as a world superpower. But a more fundamental and wide-ranging version of that same question is gnawing at nearly every American these days. The anxiety this pondering produces is quite possibly the only thing the right-wing Tea Party and leftist Occupy movements have in common.

The impulse of Tea Party types is to look for a rewind button that could return the country to an earlier time when parents could rest assured that their kids were going to have it better than they did. Their search is doomed. What is past is past. Change is inevitable. Their yearning for a return to some nostalgized yesteryear is disfiguring the Republican Party and warping the country's future.

Those drawn to the Occupy movement also are seething over the stolen dream. But their response to the fears they share with the tea partiers is totally different. They are putting their finger on what George Packer called the "broken contract."[2] For 30 years after the end of World War II, America grew together. Now we are growing apart.[3]

The battle cry of the occupiers is "We Are The 99%," condensing to bumper-sticker length the fundamental truth of the broken social contract in America. For the last 30 years, the top 1% has cleaned up and most of the rest of the population has been set adrift. The reason is simple. The top 1% has commandeered our democracy over the past three decades. They've bought the politicians and now own our government. Which permits them to rape and pillage the country while the masses are left with an unsteady present and an even more uncertain future. You have to be pushing the century mark to remember a time when income and wealth were as unequally distributed in America as it is now. Economic benefits are unequally distributed because political power is concentrated in fewer hands than it has been in several generations. All 99-percenters instinctively understand that.

There is a solution. **Recriminalize bribery.**

You have to go back more than a century, to the age of the robber barons, to find comparable social and economic conditions in America. The opulence of the Gilded Age led to the Panic of 1893 and a deep economic depression. It is no coincidence that bribing public officials was legal in places like Wisconsin at the time.

Wisconsin became a state in 1848. Bribing public officials was not outlawed until 1897. Ponder that for a moment. For the first half a century of statehood, bribery was lawful conduct and an accepted practice in Wisconsin, a state that went on to earn a reputation from coast to coast as a beacon of clean, open, honest government and progressive politics. The stand early Wisconsinites finally took in 1897 was followed in short order by another in 1905 banning corporate campaign contributions and election spending. Congress followed Wisconsin's lead in 1907 with the Tillman Act.

The 1897 and 1905 political reforms in our state paved the way for the remarkable 1911 legislative session. A feature article in the 2011 edition of my state's political bible, the Wisconsin Blue Book, says this: "*The year 2011 marks the centennial of what was almost certainly the greatest legislature in Wisconsin history, quite possibly in any state.*"

Wisconsin's reputation for progressive policy innovation was established by that legislature. Mighty blows were struck for workers' rights. Child labor laws and workplace protections for women were established. An industrial commission was set up to protect factory workers, and the nation's first worker's compensation system was created to compensate injured laborers. Insurance reforms were enacted, and a state life insurance plan established. Those weren't the only trails blazed by the 1911 legislature. The nation's first vocational, technical and adult education system was instituted. The first system of taxation based on ability to pay—the progressive income tax—was another 1911 creation. Add to the list sweeping railroad regulations and a comprehensive corrupt practices act that was a national model and served as a foundation upon which ethics laws were built from one end of the country to the other.[4]

Of course, it's highly unlikely that the actions of the 1911 legislature would have happened without the reforms of 1897 and 1905. Lawmakers acted in the public interest and advanced the common good because they were free to do so. They no longer were legally bribed. They no longer were owned by the railroad, timber and oil barons of their age.

For those of us living in Wisconsin today, all of this was our inheritance. An inheritance we have squandered, largely because we have allowed bribery to become legal again.

Oh, old-fashioned bribery remains a crime here. Today's legal bribes aren't called bribes. Now they're called campaign contributions. Makes this grimy business sound charitable. Downright philanthropic. That's a big part of the reason why they are so accepted. But the game's exactly the same as it was back in the days of the robber barons.

Different versions of this same story, more or less, could be told for every state in the union. With the shape our country is in, it is inescapably apparent that we've been pretty lousy stewards of the rich inheritance we were given by those who came before us. What we are fixing to pass on to my son's generation is not the America I want him to inherit. It is damaged goods.

We all should have known better. It's been more than 30 years, but I still remember sitting in economics classes in college and listening to more than one of my professors say with a straight face that America's economy was collapse-proof because of monetary and fiscal policy tools and regulatory protections that didn't exist when the country descended into the Great Depression.

Seemed to make sense at the time. But their instruction looks flimsy against the backdrop of Great Recession calamity. Those professors failed to account for the possibility that bought-and-paid-for politicians might one day tear down the post-Depression-era walls between banking, investment and insurance companies. They had not yet heard of and could not imagine hedge funds, derivatives, subprime mortgages, credit default swaps, mortgage-backed securities, collateralized debt obligations and other such financial flim-flam. And they seriously erred in placing so much faith in the infallibility of the Fed and the public-spiritedness of the Congress and White House.

College professors aren't the only ones who should have known better. That goes for all of us. We should have gotten to know Charles Ponzi better when he was among us the first time so we could recognize him when he came our way again. Sure enough he did return, as Bernie Madoff. Ponzi wasn't noticed until after Madoff made off with tens of billions of dollars of other people's money. Ivan Boesky and Michael Milken came again too. Not many of us remember them, and even fewer can identify their successors who went on to haunt Wall Street and wreck the national economy.

Even the best and brightest among us—from college professors and high-ranking public officials to captains of industry and the media intelligentsia—are living proof of what a comic strip told us about ourselves over 40 years ago. We have met the enemy and he is us.

So here we all sit... at kitchen tables or on living room sofas or in coffee shops... agonizing over how our kids are possibly going to make it in this world without a hell of a lot more going for them than a high school diploma, but utterly at a loss for how to get them what they need without either leaving our own finances in ruin or them buried under a mountain of debt. In Anywhere USA, moms and dads are anguishing over how this generation of young people might wind up being the first in our country's history not to be better off than their parents. It's increasingly difficult to see how kids will have any shot at a middle-class existence without education or training beyond high school, but equally hard to see how paying for college is affordable.

Nothing shapes today's politics more than the widely shared fear that the American Dream is being downsized, especially for our kids and grandkids. Yet despite the growing anxiety over the increasingly uncertain pathway to the middle class, neither Democrats nor Republicans have offered much of anything to allay the fears that will define our politics for years to come. A high school diploma clearly doesn't cut it anymore. Where are the voices saying it's time to extend the promise of free public education beyond high school? Where are the voices saying higher education and advanced vocational training needs to be as accessible and affordable in the twenty-first century as elementary and secondary education were made in the twentieth?

Politicians are not saying this kind of thing for the same reason they are not talking about poverty or the gender gap or the challenges facing farm country or urban decay. They are not saying it because they are not being paid to say it.

Big political donors aren't demanding an American Dream agenda because that dream hasn't turned into a nightmare for them or their children or grandchildren the way it has for so many Americans. And they sure aren't clamoring for a twenty-first century version of the push for expansion of educational opportunity witnessed in the 1900s. They already can afford the finest private schooling for their offspring. Unlike the captains of industry of earlier generations who understood that the success of their enterprises depended on a well-trained workforce, today's industrialists have less need for labor in their highly computerized and roboticized operations. And in today's highly mobile society and global economy, they can get what labor they need from anywhere. Cheap, adequately skilled labor will either come to them, or they can quite easily relocate to where such a workforce is to be found. This new world order has, among many other things, caused a loss of self interest in making sure that young people in Wisconsin or Kansas or any other particular spot on the world map are prepared to compete economically. Big political donors can afford to let someone else worry about the education of other people's kids.

This dynamic is not just conceptual; there are tangible real-world manifestations. Not a single new state university campus has been created in Wisconsin since 1968. But since 1994, my state has built eight new prisons and purchased a ninth that was built by a private company on speculation, added hundreds of beds to existing correctional facilities and shipped inmates to five different states to deal with overcrowding. We stopped investing in success and started paying more and more for failure instead.

Our elected representatives aren't talking about these misdirected priorities because the donor class is not interested in hearing such talk.

You could say Atlas shrugged. Then he mugged us.

While more and more of our public treasury was going to pay for punishment, Wisconsin embarked on a new educational experiment in 1990 with the creation of the Milwaukee Parental School Choice Program. An unlikely alliance of big business interests and a collection of mostly African American school reform advocates sold the governor and legislature on the idea of siphoning money away from public schools to provide families with vouchers to pay tuition at private and parochial schools.

Voucher backers emphasized the program was only for Milwaukee and only for poor families. Amid great fanfare, the program was hyped as a way to boost the academic performance of economically disadvantaged students, close the racial achievement gap, and create a competitive educational marketplace that would breed innovation and drive system change.

More than two decades after Milwaukee's program—the first of its kind in the nation—was started, the promised results have yet to materialize. Test scores show students getting vouchers to attend private schools are doing no better than public school students[5] and, by some measures, are actually doing worse.[6] The promise of innovation and system change has not been fulfilled either. Twenty-three years after the voucher program's launch, Milwaukee schools were alone in failing to meet expectations on statewide school report cards.

Still, Milwaukee's program was opened up to middle-class as well as poor families, and was expanded to nearby Racine. Not even the revelation that two-thirds of students participating in the voucher program had already been attending a private school without the help of taxpayer dollars[7] could take the wind out of the initiative's sails.

Neither the disappointing test scores nor the news that the program was really just providing a taxpayer-funded subsidy for families who already had the means to send their children to private school caused lawmakers to consider ending or at least scaling back the voucher boondoggle.

No, they didn't end the program. They expanded it statewide. On what grounds? What's good for nothing in Milwaukee is good for the entire state?

Actually, Wisconsin politicians had 97 million reasons for doing what they did. That's how many dollars pro-voucher interests gave the governor and legislators who approved the program's expansion. Interests opposed to school privatization donated $10.5 million.[8] It was an easy call. Anything that good for campaign coffers has to be good for the entire state.

This is what our republic has come to. Its survival—and the American Dream's—depends on one thing over all others. Making bribery a crime again.

CHAPTER 3
MASS HOMELESSNESS

You are a liberal. Or a progressive, or whatever term is in vogue at the moment. Republicans make you insane. But the Democrats constantly let you down. You think of going with the Green Party. Visions of wasted votes and Nader-like spoiler candidacies dance in your head. That road leads nowhere. So now where do you turn?

You are a conservative. Democrats give you nightmares. But Republicans never deliver that limited government they promise. You want to believe their rhetoric, but then there's that inconvenient reminder, like the time in 2002 when a Republican president approved the biggest expansion of the federal government in 50 years, signing a bill sponsored by a top Republican congressional leader and over a hundred of his GOP colleagues.[1] Drats. Guess you'll have to silence that inner voice that keeps saying you are too smart, too sensible and too sane for the Tea Party.

You are a moderate. That doesn't mean you are always in the middle of the road, mind you. You are conservative about some things, liberal about others. But you fancy yourself an independent. Makes you part of the biggest bloc of voters in America. So why then do you feel so alone, so powerless? You don't think much of the Democrats.

MIKE McCABE

And you could take or leave the Republicans. You vote for one side and end up feeling snookered. So you vote for the other side the next time. Snookered again. And again.

Welcome to the ranks of the politically homeless. You've got lots of company. This population makes up a larger proportion of the whole of society than at any time in some 70 years.[2] This is no accident. Nor is it sustainable.

It is no accident because both major parties currently are blind to common threads that could be used to knit together segments of society that for the time being are torn apart. It is not sustainable because broad and deep public disenchantment with both parties creates a vacuum and vacuums never last forever in democracies.

Today both the Democrats and Republicans are captive parties that cater to narrow interest groups. Neither is seen as working for the benefit of the whole country. Which is why it's been three-quarters of a century since so many people have refused to align with either major party.

At similar moments in our nation's past, transformational forces have risen up and challenged the major parties to either adapt or perish. Sometimes they've adapted as waves of reform washed over them. Other times unsustainable conditions led to major party re-alignment. Another such moment approaches.

There are common threads available to any politician or political party with a hankering for sewing. When the time comes—and it will come—when the benefits of uniting finally outweigh the re-wards of dividing, the sewing should start where the rips are most evident.

Nowhere are the rips more conspicuous than in the economy. Today we have two economies. One for the powerful and privileged that works really well for them. And another for everyone else that leaves much to be desired. This is the result of deliberate policy choices.

The Republicans may have given us trickle down, but this reverse Robin Hood philosophy has ruled over our economy for more than three decades, meaning both Democratic and Republican administrations and both Democratic and Republican majorities in Congress embraced it. In any case, it hasn't worked. It hasn't made our economy more prosperous. It hasn't made us less vulnerable to globalization and the accompanying outsourcing and offshoring of American jobs. It hasn't filled everyone's cup. All it's done is further divide us, creating more pronounced class disparities and more intense concentration of wealth at the top. All it's done is make the rich richer, the poor poorer, and the middle class an endangered species.

Democrats bristle at the suggestion they've jumped on the trickle-down bandwagon. But for well over 30 years now the Democrats have failed to offer a compelling alternative. Democrats have served up their own version of oasis economics. A few are offered refuge from the desert—and plenty to drink—while most are left stranded and thirsty. This is why Democrats have lost the support of some of the poorest among us.

Moving toward a one-for-all economy could start with a decisive move away from corporate welfare. One of the Republicans' most beloved figures completed his transformation from lightweight actor to national political colossus in 1976 by spinning a fictitious yarn about a "welfare queen" on the south side of Chicago with 80 names, 30 addresses and 12 Social Security cards who was collecting veterans benefits for four nonexistent deceased husbands as well as other public aid that brought her tax-free income to over $150,000 a year. Ronald Reagan's mythology obscured the reality that by far the biggest component of the welfare state is the flow of government assistance to the nation's corporate welfare kings that dwarfs what those stigmatized by the "welfare queen" label could ever hope to see.[3]

Trickle-down economics is built on a hoax the Democrats have never bothered to expose much less seek to dismantle, namely the fraudulent "supply-side" theory that eventually was renounced even by one of its principal architects.[4] The idea that economic growth is driven by supply and not demand defies common sense. You can bribe industrialists all you want to build factories and make things, but if there is no one wanting to buy what they're selling, those factories will be shuttered in no time.

Trying to induce big companies to create jobs through corporate tax giveaways and other government subsidies never seems to produce the jobs and the booming economy the political hype suggests it will. What it has done is subsidize the movement of jobs overseas. Companies take the handouts, pad their bottom lines, and still move operations abroad. What it also has done is create an unsavory competition between states—one state lowers its corporate taxes or offers a package of taxpayer-funded inducements, another goes lower on taxes and higher on subsidies, a third offers an even sweeter deal, each keeps trying to outdo the other—in a race to the bottom.

Both political parties are racing. In Wisconsin—with its small population and an economy in the bottom tier of U.S. states—over 5,100 grants and low-interest loans worth more than $947 million were doled out to businesses under three governors—Republicans Tommy Thompson and Scott McCallum and Democrat Jim Doyle—by the Department of Commerce.[5] As these "investments" were being made, job growth in the state slowed. Shortly after all this money was spent unemployment spiked.[6] Where the money went appeared more aimed at boosting the politicians' fortunes than the economy's. Applicants for state assistance who were campaign contributors received eight times as much aid as non-contributors.[7]

Doyle's successor, Governor Scott Walker, was among those unimpressed with the results produced by the state commerce department. After he was elected in 2010, Walker blew it up. He replaced the agency with a new part-public, part-private Wisconsin Economic Development Corporation. The WEDC had burned through more than $80 million in a matter of months before a state audit exposed how the agency had lost track of millions of dollars' worth of loans and grants, had given money to ineligible recipients, and had no idea how many jobs its aid had helped create.[8]

While it is lucrative business for the politicians, corporate welfare doesn't help the rest of us because economic growth is driven by demand, not supply. Inasmuch as government is capable of promoting commercial activity, it can only do so by putting money in the pockets of consumers. When consumers have money to spend, you can count on capitalists to produce a supply to meet the demand. Markets will be established, factories will be built, products will be made, services will be rendered, if there's a profit in it.

Despite the fact that trickle-down economics based on this highfalutin supply-side theory has made the American economy weaker rather than stronger and has only produced historic levels of economic inequality and massive concentration of income and wealth in the hands of the few at the top, the Democrats have not countered with a demand-side alternative.

How hard can it be? Hell, any farmer knows that if you've got cows and pigs and chickens, you can't just feed the cows and hope some nourishment trickles down—splatters is more like it—to the pigs and chickens. All of the animals need to be fed. Call it farmer economics for crying out loud and get busy putting some common sense policies behind the brand.

What if the hundreds of millions of dollars we are pouring down the corporate welfare rat hole every year here in Wisconsin and the billions wasted nationally were rerouted instead into an effort to wipe out student debt? We have an entire generation of college graduates who are putting off buying houses or steering clear of car purchases because they are mired in school debt. Erase that debt and you don't think home builders and car makers and dealers would scale up to accommodate the resulting rise in consumer demand?

That's just one off-the-cuff idea of how demand-side economics might work. Surely you can think of many others.

Creating a one-for-all economy requires one-for-all taxation. Face it, we now have two tax systems. One for those who make big campaign donations and can afford $250-an-hour lobbyists to work the

MIKE McCABE

corridors of power to get them write-offs and loopholes to jump through. And another for the rest of us. When you total up all state and local taxes in Wisconsin and in most states, the bottom 20% pays the highest percentage of their incomes in taxes and the top 1% pays the lowest.[9] Many if not most in our society don't want new taxes, but broad agreement can be found on the idea that everyone should pay the ones we've already got.

The problem is that there is no political household at the moment that offers hospitality to the many if not most in our society.

So the search for housing is on. Actually, it's been on for some time now.

Back in 2005, "Casino Jack" Abramoff was still riding high on K Street, and his audacious behavior and conscience-free deal making symbolized the modern lobbying trade in Washington. In 2005 Abramoff was still a year away from being sentenced to six years in federal prison for conspiracy to bribe public officials, mail fraud and tax evasion.[10] Wisconsin's State Capitol was swarming with lobbyists too. None as flamboyant as Casino Jack, but clearly the lobbying business was changing at the state level. It was fast being Washingtonized.

Despite the bad name the profession has earned, there is nothing intrinsically wrong with lobbying. After all, it is fundamentally an exercise rooted in the First Amendment right to petition the government that belongs to all citizens. I have worked as a lobbyist, first on education issues in the mid- to late-1990s and later on democracy and political reform issues.

It did not take a schooled eye to notice that a caste system was developing in Wisconsin's lobbying corps. Out of 800-some lobbyists working the halls of the State Capitol, only two dozen or so really mattered. They were the ones representing clients who supplied large sums of money for election campaigns. You could see them being ushered into the governor's office or the Assembly speaker's parlor while a flock of lower-caste advocates milled around in the hallways hoping to get a word in edgewise.

Like so many who were trying to convey the concerns of groups of people not given to making large political donations, I was accustomed to milling about. One time a state senator I had been trying unsuccessfully to reach emerged from a committee hearing and motioned to me to follow him. He made a beeline for the men's restroom. I hesitated at the door as he went in, but again he motioned to me to follow. He bellied up to a urinal and asked what I wanted him to know. I started to talk, but stopped when he let out a low groan. Judging from the expression on his face, he seemed in considerable pain, as if trying to pass a kidney stone. Feeling incredibly awkward, I gamely tried continuing to convey my message until another moan of discomfort from the senator made me pause again. I muttered a few more sentences despite feeling like a total idiot, and he finally backed away from the urinal and zipped up. He thanked me for the information and hurried back to the committee room.

What has made lobbying the despised profession it has become is not the lobbying itself. It is the marriage of lobbying and campaign fundraising. When I first worked in the Capitol as a legislative aide in the Assembly in the early 1980s, it was remarkably inexpensive to run for that state office. In a contested election in a competitive district, a winning campaign would cost you $6,000 or $8,000. Lobbyists didn't deliver bundles of checks. They didn't promise to arrange fundraisers. Their currency was information. Their success depended on their ability to make a persuasive case for the policies they promoted.

By 2005, spending in state Assembly elections in battleground regions was easily into six figures, and it was reaching seven figures for state Senate contests and eight for statewide races for offices like governor. Lobbyists were less and less valued for being good information providers and more and more valued for being political matchmakers. The favored ones ran what amounted to dating services that hooked up deep-pocketed donors with money-hungry politicians. The rest in the lobbying corps were outcasts.

Reflecting on this caste system and the Capitol culture in 2005, I got the idea of trying to organize a statewide citizen assembly to be held on January 4—the day after Wisconsin's newly elected legislature was sworn in. My group, the Wisconsin Democracy Campaign, joined with several other grassroots organizations to sponsor what we decided to call the People's Legislature.[11] The idea was that Wisconsin had a legislature that belonged to the lobbyists and their special interest clients, and the people ought to have one of their own.

Our goal was to get 804 people to take part—one more than the number of paid lobbyists working the halls of the Capitol at the time. I can't tell you how many people told me we wouldn't get 100 people to come on a weekday right after the holidays. Over 1,100 people showed up. We took the show on the road in the weeks that followed, first to La Crosse in the western part of the state and then north through a two-foot snowstorm to the small resort town of Cable, which is best known for hosting the American Birkebeiner cross country ski race. We held another assembly in the Green Bay area and one in Milwaukee. Unexpectedly large crowds greeted us at every stop.

My rather puny idea of a one-day event where regular citizens outnumbered the Capitol lobbyists had grown into something that was part barnstorming shadow legislature and part grassroots organizing network. At the assemblies we held, everyone was given the chance to have their say. As you can imagine, just about every issue under the sun was raised, from concerns isolated to one locality or region to personal axes that needed grinding.

Everywhere we went, we found a hunger for change. The issues that were on people's minds varied from place to place, but a common thread ran through all the concerns. People had lost faith in their elected officials. They didn't believe their representatives were representing them. They didn't say they were politically homeless, but they certainly expressed feeling that way.

A big issue in the north at the time was the construction of a gigantic electric power transmission line. Folks up north were worried about the effects of stray voltage and how having this big extension cord running through their back yards would change the pristine landscape and affect the tourism industry that was the region's economic lifeblood. Members of the lobbyists' legislature weren't listening. They said everyone benefits from cheap electricity.

Communities like Monroe and Stoughton were fighting Wal-Mart. They didn't want their communities to be indistinguishable from every other town in America. But they had no voice in the lobbyists' legislature. They were told everyone benefits from low prices.

In Milwaukee, we learned that 59% of African American men couldn't find work. In the 1930s, 25% unemployment was called the Great Depression. What do you call 59%? Legislators weren't calling it anything. They weren't discussing it.

Young people came to say that college tuition was on course to rise more than 50% in just four years. But there was no debate about access to higher education in the lobbyists' legislature. Others pointed out that every lake in Wisconsin was contaminated with mercury. Yet those in control of the legislature weren't cutting mercury emissions. They were pushing for more environmental deregulation.

Our assemblies were getting attention. Stories about the gatherings started showing up on the front pages of newspapers around the state. TV cameras and radio microphones were showing up too. We were attracting new followers by the day. Ed Thompson, the mayor of the small town of Tomah and the brother of longtime Wisconsin Governor Tommy Thompson, and who had made a bid for governor himself as a Libertarian in 2002, joined us. So did disaffected Republicans and disenchanted Democrats, and onetime Green Bay businessman and onetime chamber of commerce president Paul Linzmeyer, and former University of Wisconsin regent and utility executive Nino Amato.

MIKE McCABE

They weren't all bathing in stray voltage. They didn't all have a mom-and-pop shop that had been run out of business by a Wal-Mart supercenter. They weren't all unemployed black men. They weren't all college age. They didn't all have kids with stunted IQs from eating poisoned fish or asthma from breathing dirty air.

But they all had something in common with the people in Cable, and the local merchants in Monroe, and the college students, and the jobless black man. They understood that something was going haywire in our political system.

No matter where you live in America, you have a great deal in common with the members of our People's Legislature. None of them make big campaign donations. Neither do you. They don't have lobbyists prowling the halls of the Capitol on their behalf. Neither do you. It doesn't matter what you think should be at the top of the government's to-do list. It doesn't matter what's at the top of mine. If we're politically homeless, none of us is going to get what we want or need.

Deep down, they understand—and so do you—that it is illogical to expect clean air and clean water to come from dirty politics. It is unrealistic to think that policies promoting health and wellness will spring from a sick government. Work for the jobless never will be on the minds of ethically impaired and morally bankrupt professional politicians whose primary concern is their own job security. They'll think of the well-to-do every time.

Much to my surprise, the people who participated in our assemblies did what elected officials never seem able to do. After much venting, they set aside their pet causes and their parochial issues, and came together around an agenda aimed at rooting out corruption in Wisconsin government and winning some achievable political reforms. In his brilliant 2011 book *Republic, Lost* Larry Lessig quotes Thoreau's observation about how there always seems to be a thousand striking at the branches of evil for every one striking at the root. Participants in our assemblies must have identified a thousand branches, but without much prompting decided to hack away at some roots. They got behind an idea to abolish the state elections and ethics boards that had become captives of the political establishment and replace them with a new politically independent watchdog agency.

By October of 2005, our tour of the state culminated with a rally at the Capitol for the reform of the way Wisconsin's ethics code is enforced. Days after the rally, the state Senate passed the ethics enforcement reform bill. The initial euphoria of that victory faded and the reality of the lengthy legislative process and all of its hurdles set in. There must be a thousand ways to kill a bill, but only one way to pass it. Legislators employed some of those thousand ways, and ran out the clock on the session without passing the ethics bill in both houses and putting it on the governor's desk.

Amazingly, the frustration everyone felt did not take the wind out of the effort's sails. Energy and resolve remained high. The push continued. When the lobbyists' legislators refused to hold public hearings, the People's Legislature held its own "public telling" and packed a Capitol hearing room to beyond capacity.

Eventually, we had won so convincingly in the court of public opinion that pressure on lawmakers to act built to a crescendo. In a hastily arranged special session in January 2007, the ethics bill was passed by both houses of the legislature and signed into law by the governor. That reform produced a new Government Accountability Board that the Moritz School of Law at The Ohio State University later deemed a national model for nonpartisan election administration and enforcement of ethics, campaign finance and lobbying laws.[12]

Next our little engine that could set its sights on the reform of state Supreme Court elections. In 2007 those elections were turned into auctions, with $6 million spent on that year's contest—more than four times as much as Wisconsin had ever seen spent on a high court race.[13] The "Impartial Justice Act" we all got behind became a reality in 2009, overhauling the way Supreme Court elections are financed.

We felt good about the impact our efforts had made and sensed we were on to something even bigger, but little did we know then that the law would be in effect for all of one election—and even then only at half strength as a key component of the law got hung up in a court challenge—before being repealed by Governor Walker and his allies who took control of state government in the 2010 election.

Our People's Legislature did make a dent in the problem. It won one reform and lost another it had initially won. But, in any case, the People's Legislature did not create a people's legislature. It gave some politically homeless people a way to channel their energy for a time. It may have even helped their voices be heard to some extent. But it did not put an end to political homelessness. Holding some rallies won't do that. Passing a reform law or two can't do that. Doing that requires a party.

Reasons abound why Wisconsin—like all of America—has gone blind to political corruption. Among them are the pathologies evident in the major political parties. Belonging to a political party used to be like joining a club. Now it's more like getting caught up in a cult.

The frightening characteristics of religious cults are on prominent display in the two major parties. Even in a state like Wisconsin with its long history of independent politics and maverick politicians, party leaders now enforce an unwritten rule forbidding lawmakers and their staffs from socializing or otherwise fraternizing with members of the opposing party. When I was an Assembly aide, I shared an office with a woman named Linda Weiler. Years later, she was married and became Linda Narveson and must have worked 35 years or more at the Capitol, serving as an assistant to a collection of Assembly Republicans. Shortly before she passed away some years ago, I ran into Linda and she let me know she had just retired. She told me she knew it was time for her to go when she was summoned into the Assembly speaker's office and reprimanded for being seen walking on the Capitol Square with a Democratic staffer over the lunch hour. The two hadn't been talking politics. They were just getting some fresh air. That was enough to make a blot on Linda's work record.

Rank-and-file legislators are told what to think and what to say. Party leaders feed members "talking points" that at first seem innocuous enough but after a while resemble indoctrination in a terrifying group-think that rationalizes corrupt or even criminal behavior. Members who do not walk lockstep are first stripped of choice committee assignments or otherwise punished. If that does not get them to fall in line, more pliable replacements are recruited.

The leaders of the major political parties who populate Wisconsin's state legislature and our nation's Congress are not remotely representative of the people. These bosses are obsessed with who's right and who's left. If they spent half as much time thinking about what's right and wrong, Wisconsin would not have been visited by political corruption scandals of historic proportions[14] and Congress would not have historically low public approval ratings.[15] And the majority of citizens might not feel politically homeless, as they do now.

The people of Wisconsin and America are not as hopelessly divided as the political pundits like to claim. We all have much in common. But the party bosses thrive on playing up what distinguishes them from their political enemies, and this cult mentality leads them to ceaselessly drive wedges between groups of citizens.

There's much that needs doing if we are to restore some sense of honor to government. But while we endeavor to throw the bums out, we also need to think about creating a political home for common folks. We need a common party. One where common sense matters more than ideological purity. And one where talk of the common good is not so uncommon.

Maybe one of the existing parties will finally take notice of the public's wholesale retreat from public life, sense a growth opportunity, and make an offer the commoners can't refuse. Maybe.

MIKE McCABE

Just as likely, we're approaching one of those historic turning points that calls for the creation of something brand new and tests our capacity for democratic renewal.

Either way, the near future promises to be exhilarating... or petrifying, depending on how you take to social upheaval. Because the status quo is not sustainable. Something's got to give.

What if common folks with some common sense start practicing uncommon politics? What happens if neighbors challenge neighbors to house the politically homeless? In a state the size of Wisconsin, if they win over 10,000 people or even 50,000 people, the effort would likely fall flat. But what if they were able to capture the hearts and minds of 500,000 or a million? At least one of the major parties and maybe both would have to evolve or perish. Wisconsin politics would be dramatically altered. Given how people are feeling about our politics and our government and both major political parties, it could happen here. It could happen anywhere in America.

You may say I am a dreamer. But I'm not the only one.

CHAPTER 4
DEMOCRACY DISCONNECTED

Fallout from the U.S. Supreme Court's 1976 money-equals-speech ruling in *Buckley v. Valeo* and the 2010 decision in *Citizens United v. Federal Election Commission* allowing unlimited election spending by corporations and other interest groups has drifted across the entire country. But nowhere has the madness of the modern political arms race caused a greater shock to the system than in Wisconsin.

After all, Wisconsin was home to Bill Proxmire. For 32 years, the man known to people from every nook and cranny of Wisconsin simply as "Prox" was sent to Washington to represent the state in the U.S. Senate. He succeeded the red-baiting, witch-hunting Joe McCarthy and did not bite his tongue about "Tail Gunner Joe," calling him a "disgrace to Wisconsin, to the Senate, and to America."[1] Prox impressed blue-collar folks with his strong work ethic, setting the record for consecutive roll call votes cast in the Senate, a whopping 10,252 between April 20, 1966 and October 18, 1988, breaking the previous record of 2,941 by Senator Margaret Chase Smith of Maine.

He was best known for his legendary frugality (over the years he returned more than $900,000 from his Senate office allowances to the U.S. Treasury), his tireless handshaking (he delighted in showing off the new blisters and old callouses he got from pressing the flesh) and, of course, his flair for exposing wasteful government spending and lampooning it with his "Golden Fleece Awards." The very first one was awarded in 1975 to the National Science Foundation for funding an $84,000 study on why people fall in love. Others over the years went to the Justice Department for conducting a study on why prisoners wanted to get out of jail, the National Institute of Mental Health for a study of a Peruvian brothel, and the Federal Aviation Administration for studying the "physical measurements of 432 airline stewardesses, paying special attention to the 'length of the buttocks.'"[2]

Just as amazing was his approach to campaigning. Proxmire accepted no contributions and spent less than $300 on his bids for office. In his last run in 1982, Prox registered only $145.10 in campaign costs. But he was consistently returned to office by huge majorities, including 71% of the vote in 1970, 73% in 1976 and 65% in 1982, when he ran for a fifth and final full six-year term.[3]

Bill Proxmire was the embodiment of Wisconsin's tradition of clean and open government. Prox's name will forever be attached to the state's proud progressive past and his memory will always evoke images of independence and integrity.

In the span of a single generation, Wisconsin has gone from a place where it was possible to run successfully for statewide office for $145 to one that has seen $81 million spent to decide who sits in the governor's office.[4] The transformation of Wisconsin's electoral landscape and accompanying loss of innocence did not happen all of a sudden. It was creeping corruption.

Caucuses. They sounded harmless enough.

In most political circles, caucuses are groupings of like-minded legislators. In Iowa, they are a time-honored method of voting. But in Wisconsin, they were something else.

These obscure state offices were established as part of 1960s and 1970s reforms to strengthen the capacity of the legislature to act independently of the executive branch and to become a more truly coequal branch of state government.

Four of these offices were created—one for each party in both houses of the legislature. They were to do research on issues and write policy papers and provide legislative analysis. Lawmaking is an inherently political undertaking, so gradually the caucuses evolved to take on a more overtly political role. Caucus staffers were doing speech writing for members, and were producing taxpayer-funded constituent newsletters whose mailing was timed as close to election time as possible for maximum political benefit.

Eventually the caucuses morphed into full-time election campaign headquarters. The public employees working in these government offices with equipment and materials furnished by the taxpayers were building voter lists, recruiting candidates, soliciting campaign contributions, selecting political consultants, producing campaign materials, doing opposition research (the polite term in the industry for digging up dirt on political enemies), building campaign organizations and doing election-related field work.

These morphed caucuses were a lot of things—incubators of political corruption, for starters—but harmless they were not.

These offices were using taxpayer money to break the law. A *Wisconsin State Journal* investigation in 2001 revealed widespread use of state offices, equipment and resources by caucus employees—on state time and the taxpayers' dime—to campaign for state legislative candidates in obvious violation of state ethics and campaign finance laws.[5]

The caucuses were costing taxpayers about $4 million a year and were being run by the four legislative leaders—the Senate majority and minority leaders and the Assembly speaker and minority leader. When the *State Journal* exposés about flagrant misuse of taxpayer money for secret, illegal campaigning filled the front pages for weeks on end, the legislative leaders offered a few weasel words, some lame double talk, but mostly they played dumb. Despite the fact the caucuses were operating under their direct supervision, they claimed they had no knowledge of any illegal activity.

The leaders stonewalled even as the investigation expanded to include not only the misuse of public offices, illegal campaign contributions and collusion between one of the caucuses and a supposedly independent campaign committee, but also revelations that one caucus violated the state's open records law by destroying or hiding documents sought by the newspaper.

The caucuses were using taxpayer money to break the law. But worse yet, they were using that money to steal democracy. Thanks to the caucuses, voters got fewer choices at the ballot box. In 1970, before the caucuses were turned into the taxpayer-funded campaign headquarters they are today, there were no uncontested legislative races in Wisconsin. Every incumbent had at least a major party opponent. In the 2000 elections, 40% of incumbent legislators were unopposed.

That's because these leadership-controlled machines supplanted local political party organizations. Local parties have an interest in having someone on the ballot in every community to carry the party's banner. The legislative leaders only care about a handful of battleground districts that will decide which party controls the legislature. So they funneled caucus resources only to those races that mattered to them.

Thanks to the caucuses, Wisconsinites got less responsive representation. Wisconsin once had one of the most decentralized legislatures in the country—a legislature full of maverick spirit. Today, we have one of the nation's most centrally controlled legislatures. You'd think in a state as diverse as Wisconsin, newly elected legislators would come to Madison with agendas as unique as the communities they were elected to serve. But if you look at the candidates' campaign literature and watch their ads, you see so much uniformity that it's hard to believe it's coincidental.

That's because the caucuses gave the legislative leaders control over the campaign machinery as well as the purse strings, giving them the ability to hand-pick politicians of their choosing to serve with them—actually, *under* them—in the legislature.

The caucuses were anti-democratic in the extreme. This system turned the legislature into a gated community. Only favored insiders can get in, and once they're in, the system keeps them there. The leaders don't anoint independent-minded candidates, they recruit and groom loyal followers who'll remain acutely aware of who's buttering their bread. The result is that we got legislators who were more responsive to the powers-that-be in the Capitol than to the people in the communities they are elected to represent.

Ironically, the taxpayer-funded caucuses were fiercely defended even by those legislators who opposed the use of any tax dollars for public financing of state election campaigns. Campaign reforms proposed by both Republicans and Democrats to offer public grants to candidates who agree to limit campaign spending had price tags about the same as the expense of operating the caucuses. But anti-reform legislators ridiculed public financing as "welfare for politicians" or "socialized campaigning." Those same politicians had no problem illegally spending the taxpayers' money on the caucuses that worked to get them re-elected. It was public financing, sure enough, but only for the incumbents and for challengers hand-picked by the legislative leaders.

The revelations in the media did turn into a secret John Doe investigation that involved local, state and federal law enforcement authorities. The probe ended up yielding nearly four dozen state and federal felony charges against five current or former state legislators and one Capitol staffer as well as misdemeanor charges against another legislator and several other staffers. All of the lawmakers and staffers were convicted. Two of the former legislators received jail sentences and two others were sentenced to prison, although one of them was granted a new trial on a technicality and eventually reached a plea agreement dismissing felony charges and accepting a

$5,000 fine after more than eight years of legal maneuvering. All of their political careers were ended, and legislation was enacted abolishing the caucus offices.[6]

But the damage was done. Wisconsin's political culture was changing. The caucuses were gone and so were the legislative leaders who oversaw them. But the genie that had been released could not easily be stuffed back in the bottle.

Wisconsin used to be known for its squeaky clean politics and open, honest government. That reputation was the byproduct of stratospherically high ethical standards. Our state was in the vanguard of the war on corruption when bribery was banned here in 1897, and Wisconsin blazed another new trail when corporate electioneering was prohibited in 1905. Standards were further raised with the enactment of the Corrupt Practices Act in 1911. Primary elections were pioneered here, opening up the process of nominating candidates for public office, turning over to voters a task previously performed by party bosses in smoke-filled rooms.

The 1970s brought new waves of ethics and campaign finance reform, most notably the establishment of a comprehensive ethics code that included the nation's strictest gift ban prohibiting lobbyists from giving "anything of value" to state officials. That same decade Wisconsin became one of the first states to start publicly financing election campaigns.

In 1978 Wisconsin's high standards were on prominent display when a state senator named Henry Dorman was criminally charged for an intolerable ethical breach. The charges were eventually dismissed, but not until after voters threw him out of office and ended his political career. His crime? Charging a few personal calls to a state telephone credit card.

The way the money game in politics evolved in the next several decades has made a mockery of our ethics code. The gift ban's definition of "anything of value" does not cover the thing of greatest value to today's politicians—campaign contributions. In 1973 when the law was enacted and Bill Proxmire embodied Wisconsin politics, that probably didn't seem like much of an oversight. Today, in the age of Citizens United and Super PACs and campaigns that are glorified collection agencies for the TV stations, that omission renders the law meaningless. Wisconsin's gift ban isn't worth the paper it's written on. If you give a politician a t-shirt with your company's name on it, or a coffee mug bearing your group's logo, you are committing a crime. But it's entirely legal to write out a check for $500 or $1,000 or $10,000 and hand it to that same politician. What's more valuable to politicians—and what's more likely to influence them—the t-shirt or the check? The mug or the money?

When the history books are written, what we are living through will go down as one of the most corrupt periods in America's political history. Even in places like Illinois. Our neighbor to the south has a long history of sustained political corruption. "Governor" has long been a universally understood synonym for crooked there. Yet even in Illinois, the condition of democracy is in worse shape than it once was.

There is a sequence to how most of us process the onset of moral decay in politics. Sure, it depends on whether the change is radical, as it has been in Wisconsin, or more subtle, as in Illinois. Still, there is a sequence. First there is surprise, often accompanied by denial. Then there is anger. Then resignation.

We've grown resigned to the desecration of democracy as public elections turned into private auctions. Bill Proxmire's $145 campaigns went the way of the dinosaur in Wisconsin. Even before the U.S. Supreme Court dropped a bomb on the political landscape with its decision in the Citizens United case, my state was in the midst of a full-blown campaign arms race. In the two election cycles before the court's ruling in 2010, $124 million was spent on Wisconsin elections. After the ruling, spending more than tripled. A whopping $392 million was poured into elections in the state in the two post Citizens United election cycles.[7]

MIKE McCABE

When John Doe came back to haunt Wisconsin a decade after our caucus scandal, he found us numb. The latest investigation into political wrongdoing in my state led to criminal charges against six former aides and associates of Governor Walker—and all were convicted—for offenses ranging from illegal campaign activity by taxpayer-funded staffers (sound familiar?) and illegally laundered campaign contributions to embezzlement of funds intended to benefit veterans.[8] But Wisconsin voters did not give Walker the treatment Henry Dorman received. The governor was kept in office.[9]

Numb's the word when public involvement in the affairs of state is treated as an unwelcome intrusion as it has been in Wisconsin, where both the "public" and the "hearing" have been taken out of public hearings, as legislators and lobbyists speak first and can talk for as long as they wish while citizens are made to wait and then are frequently limited to three minutes worth of remarks—if they get called to speak at all before the meeting is adjourned.

After the rights of working people to organize were taken away, mass demonstrations that swelled to 100,000 people or more on the Capitol grounds eventually gave way to mass resignation. A circuit court judge threw out Wisconsin's infamous Act 10 on the grounds that the votes on it were held in violation of the state's open meetings law. A state Supreme Court justice who previously had been speaker of the Assembly wrote in a majority opinion that the lower court judge was wrong to rely on laws that "apply to the legislature except when the legislature says they do not."[10] His face was presumably straight when he wrote it, and his audacious holding was met with amazingly little derision. In fact, there was next to no media commentary. Even the Fourth Estate appeared numb.

In the aftermath of the massive protests in 2011, exercising the First Amendment right of citizens to peaceably assemble became a punishable offense in Wisconsin. New rules were put in place that trampled on the First Amendment right of citizens to peaceably assemble by requiring groups of more than four to obtain a permit in order to assemble at the Capitol and post bond to cover the cost of police "protection."[11] Never mind that the policy flew in the face of Wisconsin's constitution, which says citizens cannot be prevented from entering the Capitol.[12]

Recent years have been rough ones for high ethical standards in politics, and not just in Wisconsin. Just about every fundraising and spending record, broken. Smear campaigning, everywhere. Election spending restrictions, gutted. Public financing, repealed. Public faith in the system, lost. One blow after another to the body of democracy.

But the biggest blow of all to the Wisconsin way is the state of mind of most of our citizens when it comes to the political landscape. Most of us are not surprised anymore. Most of us are not mad—at least not enough to act on our anger. Most of us just shrug. Most of us are numb.

The cynical view that politics has always been like this and always will be this way is taking root in the citizenry. Holding such a view requires the holder to overlook or remain ignorant of the history of places like Wisconsin. Politics has not always been this way here. It has not always been this way in Congress. Don't forget, there have been times when the vast majority of Americans actually approved of the way Congress was doing its job. There was a time when public officials like Bill Proxmire were respected and even revered. There was a time when the smallest indiscretion by the likes of a Henry Dorman was not tolerated.

Politics is not inherently good or evil. Political culture acts as an invisible hand that guides the behavior of those who practice politics. The public has more to do with establishing that culture than public officials. We have allowed our political culture to become debased.

Democracy in our land faces greater threats than any seen in our lifetimes. Most people no longer believe they are being represented, no longer believe their voices are being heard, and no longer believe their interests are being served. Most people have good reason to feel that way. There are a great many corrupt behaviors and practices that need to be stopped. The first is our own indifference.

CHAPTER 5
THE
STILTED AGE

To find a period in American history with a concentration of power, corporate influence and political corruption comparable to today's you have to go back to the late 1800s. There was Boss Tweed and Tammany Hall. There were the robber barons. That's what they called the likes of John D. Rockefeller, Andrew Carnegie, J.P. Morgan, John Jacob Astor and Cornelius Vanderbilt. There was Mark Hanna, the Cleveland industrialist and politician who befriended Rockefeller at a young age. It was Hanna who famously said: "There are two things that are important in politics. The first is money and I can't remember what the second one is." Mark Twain coined the term "Gilded Age" to describe that corrupt era.

No doubt remains that we are reliving the Gilded Age. The only question is what name the historians will finally settle on for this latest era of rampant materialism, blatant corruption and grotesque inequality. Stilted Age has a nice ring to it, and the name fits a time when a comfortable few rest easily above the floodwaters while an afflicted many watch jobs and homes and savings and ways of life wash away.

It's odd how our nation's highest court now says corporations are people, yet today's captains of industry have never been more faceless and the companies they run have never been more inanimate. Rockefeller, Carnegie and Vanderbilt became household names in the Gilded Age. Who can name the current CEO of Exxon Mobil or who headed the investment bank Goldman Sachs or insurance giant AIG when they wrecked our economy? Which top British Petroleum exec was that again who talked of caring about the "small people" whose lives were being ruined by the oil spill in the Gulf of Mexico? If not for the Koch brothers, today's robbers would largely be nameless and faceless.

The way they acquire and wield power is harder to see, too. There was a time when efforts to keep people in their place were easily recognizable. Bondage is hard to miss. Women were chattel and blacks were slaves. Slavery and related tactics of social and economic control represent the first stage of ownership in America. The nation's royals eventually lost their moral and legal justification for employing such crude and brutal means to keep people down, but not their desire for race, class and gender superiority. So they developed a more sophisticated approach. Slavery was out, Jim Crow was in. Poll taxes and literacy tests were put in place. Give them rights, but make sure they are not equal rights. No longer violent, but still unmistakably bigoted. Call it the second stage of ownership.

The civil rights legislation of the 1960s ended Jim Crow but not the royals' discriminatory impulses. It is no coincidence that shortly after civil rights-era legislation culminated with the passage of Title IX of the Education Amendments of 1972 targeting sex discrimination, the U.S. Supreme Court took up a legal challenge to restrictions on money in politics in a case called Buckley v. Valeo. The court's money-equals-speech ruling paved the way for the onset of a third stage of ownership where the ruling class has found ways to thwart the will of the masses even while allowing the exercise of largely equal rights. Campaign donations became the smart bombs of the race and class wars. Their beauty as a tool of social and economic control is that they don't appear discriminatory because, in theory at least,

MIKE McCABE

anyone can make them. But as organized money understands, the difference between theory and practice in campaign giving is as distinct as the divisions of race and class. In this third stage, ownership of the levers of power is preserved by making political expression and participation prohibitively expensive for all but a few.

As noted in chapter 1, there are close to 900 zip codes in Wisconsin, but most of the political money comes from barely 30 of them. They are all urban or suburban, predominantly white and wealthy. A single zip code—53217 in the Milwaukee area's wealthiest "Gold Coast" suburbs—produced considerably more in campaign contributions than the state's 61 poorest zip codes combined and almost four times as much as the 15 zip codes with the largest nonwhite populations.[1]

Money from these elite donors flows to friendly candidates in every corner of the state, deciding elections hundreds of miles from where the donors live, elections in which they are not eligible to vote. It's gotten so bad that a great many legislators get more from the top-giving zip codes than from voters in their own districts. On average, Wisconsin lawmakers get two-thirds of their campaign contributions from outside the districts they represent, and a few actually get all of their money from people who cannot vote for them.[2] All the money comes from a tiny segment of society. In state elections, an elite cadre of donors amounting to just over 1% of the country's adult population makes all the donations that fuel all the spending.[3] The story is the same in federal elections.[4] The real money is coming from a fraction of 1% of the population.[5] More than a quarter of all contributions come from 1% of the 1%.[6]

Organized money's insidious power has robbed voters in most parts of the state of their ability to control their own political destiny. Long before voters ever cast a ballot, whoever is most successful in attracting money from the "giving zips" wins what amounts to a wealth primary. That pre-primary "election" weeds out any meaningful competition, leaving the people with a vote but little if any choice. The wealth primary works hand in hand with the practice of gerrymandering political boundaries described in chapter 12 to strip elections of competitiveness and render them pale imitations of democratic contests. And not just here in my state. In this regard Wisconsin is the norm nationally, not the exception.

With instruments of control at their disposal as powerful as the abuse of the redistricting process and their monopoly on political speech made possible by judicial mangling of the meaning of the First Amendment, today's ruling elites hardly need any longer to dirty their hands with flagrant attempts to deny people their right to vote. But dirty their hands they still do.

Already having secured the means to keep people down by allowing them to freely vote in elections whose results are preordained, they nevertheless take no chances. Discriminatory drug policies and the practice of racial profiling by law enforcement authorities and the resulting mass incarceration of African American males are extensions of Jim Crow. And, in 2011 and 2012 alone, more than 30 states introduced legislation or enacted laws curbing the ability to vote. Some dramatically shortened early voting opportunities. Others have passed legislation to make it harder for volunteer organizations like the League of Women Voters to register voters. Most popular among the voter suppression tactics currently in vogue is a legal requirement to show a state-issued photo ID in order to cast a ballot. In 2011 and 2012, 10 states joined Indiana and Georgia in requiring voters to show a photo ID to vote.[7]

The modern popularity of racist criminal justice policies and voter suppression tactics shows that the second stage of ownership is not a bygone era. Perhaps in a nod to third-stage sensibilities, however, voter ID laws have been sold as an election integrity measure needed to prevent voter fraud. Indiana's voter ID law survived a legal challenge when a federal judge upheld it on those grounds. New evidence later came to his attention that convinced him the purpose of Indiana's law is voter suppression, not fraud prevention. The judge publicly acknowledged his ruling was mistaken,[8] but the damage was done. Lawmakers pushing voter ID laws in places like Wisconsin claimed their proposals were modeled after Indiana's law, which had been declared constitutional.

Attorneys defending Pennsylvania's voter ID law made an awkward confession as they prepared for trial, conceding that they had no evidence of the kind of voter fraud that purportedly could be prevented by requiring voters to show government-issued photo identification in order to cast a ballot. The lawyers could produce no evidence of identity fraud in voting done in Pennsylvania or in any other state.[9]

By 2012, close to half a million Americans were facing significant barriers to obtaining the kind of ID needed to vote in their states. Among the problems is that many ID-issuing offices have limited business hours. For example, the office in Sauk City, Wisconsin is open only on the fifth Wednesday of any month. But only four months in 2012—February, May, August and October—have five Wednesdays. Getting an ID sometimes requires additional documentation that can be difficult and costly to obtain. Birth certificates are required in Wisconsin, and in our parts a copy of the certificate can cost between $8 and $25. Marriage licenses, required for married women whose birth certificates include a maiden name, can cost between $8 and $20. By comparison, the notorious poll tax—outlawed during the Civil Rights Era—cost $10.64 in current dollars.[10]

Afraid of second-stage appearances and aware that the new fraud-prevention policies look conspicuously like old racist poll taxes, officials are being creative in defending their tactics. In June 2013, the U.S. Supreme Court struck down a core provision of the Voting Rights Act of 1965 that required a number of states to get federal approval before changing their election laws. Texas was one of those states, and soon found itself in court again facing a Justice Department lawsuit seeking to get the state back under federal oversight. To win, the Justice Department had to prove intentional racial discrimination.

One of the laws in Texas that became subject to legal scrutiny was the state's ridiculously gerrymandered redistricting plan. The state offered a novel legal defense. Texas essentially pleaded guilty to discrimination, but argued it was on the basis of party, not race. "It is perfectly constitutional for a Republican-controlled legislature to make partisan districting decisions, even if there are incidental effects on minority voters who support Democratic candidates."[11]

Black and Hispanic voters in Texas and elsewhere can be forgiven for seeing deliberate efforts to crowd as many minority voters into as few districts as possible as something more than "incidental."

In North Carolina, minority voters—who incidentally tend to favor Democrats—are harmed by that state's new voting law, which includes provisions significantly limiting early voting, eliminating election-day registration during early voting, imposing a restrictive photo identification requirement for in-person voting, and prohibiting the counting of otherwise legitimate provisional ballots that are mistakenly cast in the right county, but in the wrong precinct.[12]

Taking a page from the Texas legal defense, North Carolina Republican official Don Yelton admitted a naked partisan motive behind the law, telling Comedy Central's *The Daily Show* that his state's law "is going to kick the Democrats in the butt."

Then Yelton got to those pesky incidental effects. If, while the law is hurting his political opponents, it also "hurts a bunch of lazy blacks," then "so be it."[13] If only there were a Don Yelton in every state bent on voter suppression, willing to blurt out the truth about the real motives, these kinds of laws would have been quickly exposed for what they are.

Unfortunately, most of the people in charge of government and in service to the 1% are not Don Yeltons. They can want one thing and say with perfectly straight faces they want the opposite. The great Indian independence leader Mahatma Gandhi once said "happiness is when what you think, what you say and what you do are in harmony." By that standard, I can count the number of happy politicians I've met on one hand, with fingers to spare.

Most of the politicians I've encountered over the last 30-plus years around the Capitol started out with good intentions, entering public office for mostly the right reasons. Then they start playing the game. And the game changes them.

One of the things I marvel at the most is how many of them seem largely unaware of how the game is changing them and how they are assimilating into the Capitol culture. It happens fast too. The stark difference between freshmen legislators and second-termers never ceases to amaze me.

I can't imagine there is that big of a change in how they think. Maybe there is. But more likely, a disconnection develops between what they think and what they say and do. This disconnect is the taproot of corruption. Most politicians can't see it. They're steeped in all the same stereotypes of corrupt politicians as the rest of us are. They figure if they don't look and act like Boss Tweed, they must be OK.

Therein lies the problem. Real corruption isn't as black and white as you'd think. It is painted in countless shades of gray. It doesn't present itself in the form of a familiar caricature. And it mysteriously doesn't seem to present itself at all to those who are being corrupted. It's invisible. That's the thing about corruption. Those who fall victim are almost always the last to see it.

I am not without sympathy. Elected officials are under very real and very extreme pressures. None more extreme than those that come from within. They are tugged mercilessly in different directions by competing impulses. They are damned if they do and damned if they don't. Anyone who resists assimilation into the Capitol culture risks becoming a pariah. A wet-behind-the-ears misfit. You become an easy target for the worst of all possible insults that can be hurled at a politician, namely that *you don't know how to play the game.*

On the other hand, if you go along, if you try to fit in, you have to know that there is a price to pay. And I'm not just talking about the year-round campaign fundraising, the incessant dialing for dollars. Or pretending that you actually enjoy the company of stuffed shirts and oily con men. No, the biggest toll is knowingly and willingly accepting that what you think, say and do must be negotiable. And by no means in harmony.

If this sounds to you like saying farewell to integrity—not to mention happiness, at least by Gandhi's standards—then you grasp the going price of power at the Capitol.

All of which raises the question: Why do they, *why do we*, tolerate a political culture that forces good, well-intentioned people to do this?

Power, at its current price, costs too much—for those in the corridors of power, and certainly for those outside the political arena who must live with the consequences of the morally compromised decisions made by those entrusted to govern.

It is said the first casualty of war is truth. So it is in political warfare. And the second casualty has to be shame. Once fully assimilated into today's political culture, those who fill our public stations have got shame licked. The more shameful their behavior, the more shameless they are about it. Evidently it all balances out in their minds.

If you'd rather not ponder such ethical gymnastics, you had best not dwell on recent Wisconsin political history. For a state with such a long tradition of clean, progressive government and public-spirited lawmaking like the historic actions of 1911 discussed in chapter 2, it is not a pretty picture. Government went to work building the stilts.

Just over a decade ago, while constructing a safe harbor for the 1%, the stilt builders preached public safety to the masses. With jobs vanishing by the thousands across Wisconsin, state lawmakers who were already on a prison-building binge hauled out weapons of mass distraction—concealed weapons, that is. Two-thirds of the people were telling pollster after pollster at the time that they didn't want neighbors much less strangers walking around with guns stuffed in their undies. Their "elected representatives"—eager to please the powerful gun lobby—legalized concealed carry anyway.

With books cooked Enron style to make the state budget appear balanced, the legislature turned its attention to the pressing task

MIKE McCABE

of defining marriage as a union between a husband and wife. With 600,000 in the state uninsured and countless others a pink slip away from not being able to take their kids to the doctor, state legislators moved quickly to allay the growing fear of... shopping cart theft. Since when does shopping cart theft trump job creation or budget balancing or health care reform on the public's to-do list? Since the grocers and other backers of the bill greased the legislative skids with over $1 million in campaign contributions to legislators, including nearly $184,000 to the bill's author and sponsors.

With the nation at war against terrorism, Wisconsin lawmakers must have known that fighting crime so trivial wouldn't do. So it took a helpful nudge from retail gas dealers and related businesses who gave legislators over $1.2 million to convince the legislature to broaden its anti-crime agenda to include cracking down on gas station drive-offs.

Captains of industry who showered legislators with millions in campaign contributions saw a faltering economy as a perfect opening for more deregulation of their enterprises. But they weren't born yesterday. They knew the "Business Deregulation Act" would be about as popular as Brett Favre's defection to the Vikings. So they gave their pet bill a name that set Orwell's grave to trembling—the "Job Creation Act."

To create some untold (and ultimately uncountable) number of jobs, the bill did things like allowing trout streams and lakebeds to be dredged without any opportunity for public comment or regulatory oversight. That recipe for economic development ran on for 114 pages.

Who in the legislature claimed pride of authorship? Well, no one. Legislative leaders, themselves marinated in hundreds of thousands of dollars worth of campaign donations from backers of the bill, let industry lobbyists write the bill. It wasn't the first time. Or the last. Lobbyists never used to have a hand in writing legislation in Wisconsin. Now it is common practice.

When all of the tax breaks and loopholes, pork barrel spending projects, lucrative state contracts and other favors tucked in the state
budget back in 2003 were totaled up, the cost approached $5 billion,
or nearly $1,200 for each and every taxpayer in the state.[14]

Nowhere to be found on the legislature's agenda that year was campaign finance reform. Three years after 90% of voters in a statewide
referendum said they wanted the financing of election campaigns
cleaned up, the people were still waiting for their own elected representatives to stop debating concealed weapons or the definition
of marriage or shopping cart theft long enough to do the cleaning.

The chairman of the Assembly elections committee, which controlled the fate of campaign reform in the lower house, refused to
hold a public hearing, let alone a vote, on the issue. He blamed my
group for his inaction. He told *The Capital Times* that every time
he was getting around to it, "we'd have the Democracy Campaign
do something stupid—like writing letters to the editor," that he insisted only stiffened the resolve of reform opponents. He told the
newspaper such actions were "extreme tactics."[15]

A couple of years later, at the behest of their paymasters, Wisconsin
legislators started preempting or overturning local government decisions, preventing communities from setting their own minimum
wage, regulating smoking in taverns and eateries, confiscating illegal
video gambling machines in bars, blocking the construction of high-
voltage electric power transmission lines and other utility-backed
energy projects, and establishing their own school calendars.[16]

By the decade's end they were deregulating telecommunications,
and at the beginning of the new one they were exempting glorified
loan sharks—"payday lenders" in modern parlance—from a key part
of state consumer protection laws. In 2011 they busted unions and
cut public employee compensation[17] while lavishing state largesse
on corporations.[18] In 2012, they doubled down on corporate welfare,
serving up a smorgasbord of dozens of new business tax breaks and
subsidies worth hundreds of millions of dollars.[19] They overrode local opposition to the resuscitation of iron ore mining in the Penokee

Range in the state's north woods and rewrote environmental protection laws to grease the skids for out-of-state mining interests to get cracking on a massive new mine right at the headwaters of the Bad River. It was hard not to notice that pro-mining interests made nearly $16 million in campaign donations to the governor and legislators who pushed through the mining bill, while those opposed to the project gave barely $25,000.[20]

Today's lawmakers don't need to gather ideas or take their cues from their local constituents. As of 2013, fully a third of Wisconsin legislators were members of the American Legislative Exchange Council. ALEC is one part corporate-funded dating service and one part special interest bill mill. ALEC's matchmaking forges relationships between corporate bigwigs and state lawmakers, and when the wining and dining is done the legislators are sent home with ready-to-introduce draft legislation. Records obtained about ALEC's inner workings show that it has pushed for a job description for legislators as well as a signed loyalty pledge from member lawmakers promising to put ALEC's interests first.[21]

No keen powers of observation are required to see the parallels between the nineteenth century Gilded Age and the times we live in, where a privileged few have once again been lifted above the pain and suffering inflicted on the masses. Eerie similarities abound. Differences too, of course. We are not on the tail end of an Industrial Revolution or re-experiencing post-Reconstruction upheaval. No, we have economic convulsions of our very own as our post-Industrial world continues to morph.

How *should* our economy be described? Service? Digital? Post-Human? It suffices to say that economic dislocation, occupational insecurity and financial anxiety are hallmarks of our moment, just as they were in the late 1800s. Likewise, instruments of social control and political manipulation are being put to daily use by a privileged few to establish and maintain ownership of our government and our society, just as they were at the end of the nineteenth century. But those instruments have mutated.

At the dawn of our nation, slavery and disenfranchisement were the control mechanisms. Only white male property owners had access to the ballot and, consequently, any say over affairs of state. Decades-long—no, generations-long—struggles eventually put an end to slavery and won voting rights for women, blacks and unpropertied men. But those who succumbed to the abolitionists and the suffragettes had no intention of surrendering control or relinquishing power. They relied on discriminatory election rules and the like to achieve their objective.

Then came the Equal Pay Act of 1963, the Civil Rights Act of 1964, the Voting Rights Act of 1965, the Equal Credit Opportunity Act of 1968, and the enactment of Title IX in 1972. After painful and drawn-out fights, the crude second-stage instruments of sociopolitical control were gradually swept away. But the ruling elite's sense of entitlement to political power and economic supremacy was never extinguished.

As discussed, it is hardly coincidental that the great civil rights and women's rights breakthroughs of the 1960s and 1970s were followed in short order by the 1976 Supreme Court ruling establishing that money is speech. As Roger D. Hodge wrote in an exceptionally insightful essay in the October 2010 issue of *Harper's*, campaign contributions and other forms of political spending have assumed the old exclusionary function. Only those who can afford to pay have a voice. Only those with vast wealth are truly able to control their political destiny.[22]

The massive transfer of America's wealth to the richest 1% that began in earnest in the early 1980s and has continued unabated during Republican and Democratic administrations alike is no coincidence either. As Hodge rightly points out, it was the result of a long series of policy decisions that were bought and paid for by the less than 1% of Americans who annually pour hundreds of millions of dollars into political campaigns.

In 2010 the Supreme Court radically expanded on *Buckley* and accelerated our plunge into the third-stage abyss with its ruling in the Citizens United case allowing corporations and other powerful groups to spend unlimited sums on elections. Just as the Supreme Court gamely defended and empowered the ruling elite during the first stage of ownership by ruling that people could be property, the highest court in the land is now serving third-stage masters by ruling that property can be a person.

On the surface and for the time being, the 1% appears to be riding high, economically and politically speaking. Riding roughshod might be a more apt description. They have been positively cleaning up in very recent times.

Closer inspection shows signs of desperation in high places, however. Say what you will about them, but the 1% can read the handwriting on the wall.

They can see the browning face of America and its implications for political power.[23] And they can see that this change will only accelerate in the foreseeable future, with the country's white majority becoming a minority by 2043 or thereabouts.[24]

They can see generational change coming, too. Many if not most Americans seem disinclined to turn on them, but not so with the so-called Millennials. The teens and twenty-somethings are downright disenchanted with corporate America. While older generations remain largely sold on capitalism, Pew Research shows the Millennials are actually quite warm to socialism.[25] Grim job prospects and a downsized American Dream buried under a mountain of student debt will do that.

Democracy, with its core emphasis on majority rule, is fundamentally numerical. With fast-changing demographics and generational angst working against them, the 1% is confronted with a political landscape where it will be increasingly difficult for them to numerically hold on to their privileged status as America's ruling class.

Desperate times yield extreme measures. A future marked with growing inability to win numerically explains why the 1% devotes so much energy to rigging the political game procedurally and financially. America's changing face and shifting political terrain explain the recent surge in voter suppression efforts. And it goes a long way toward explaining mass incarceration.[26]

That handwriting on the wall the 1% is reading explains why we're seeing the most brazen manipulation of political boundaries through partisan gerrymandering in living memory. It explains why the stilted ones needed an obliging Supreme Court to rule as it did in the Citizens United case. And it explains why Citizens United is not enough. They need the court to go even farther on their behalf. In April 2014, the court obliged with its ruling in *McCutcheon v. FEC* striking down the aggregate limit on campaign contributions to federal candidates and political committees.[27] There's good reason to believe further accommodations will be made.

Emerging demographic and generational realities are creating political conditions under which maintenance of the 1%'s iron grip on power is incompatible with democracy. That's why democracy is under such vicious assault.

They are ruling on borrowed time.

CHAPTER 6
AN AMERICAN CONUNDRUM

At this moment, when it has dawned on many if not most Americans that we have a bought Congress and bought legislatures, it's worth reflecting on the fact that in the Federalist Papers, one of the founding fathers (widely thought to be James Madison in this instance), writing under the pseudonym "Publius," said that Congress "ought to be dependent on the People alone"[1] and "not the rich, more than the poor."[2]

There can be no doubt anymore that Congress has competing—and conflicting—dependencies that lead its members time and time again to put the wishes of the rich ahead of the needs of everyone else. That the same is true in our state legislatures also is self-evident.

How very far we've strayed from the founders' vision.

Both major parties have strayed. Both parties are failing America. Each in its own way, but both are failing us nevertheless. Leaving voters to do a dance at election time that might be called the hate 'em all lurch.

Every election's results seem to be over analyzed and misinterpreted by the media pundits and the political class. Nearly every time we hear talk of historic political realignment. One time we are told voters are shifting dramatically to the left (as in 2006 and 2008) and another time we are told the electorate is on the move again, heading sharply to the right (as in 2010).

Voters were no more fond of Republicans in 2010 than they are today or than they were last month or last year or four years ago. And voters didn't become dyed-in-the-wool Democrats in 2006 and 2008. The vast majority of voters hate both major parties with a passion. Virtually all voters are holding their noses when they cast a ballot and feel doomed to choose between the lesser of two evils.

The Onion got it right. "Millions of Americans courageously lined up to vote yesterday despite the very real threat of electing the 112th Congress."[3] Thank God for satire. The last safe harbor for truth.

The average voter understands that their elected representatives are listening to and working for the lobbyists and their big campaign donors, not the general public. And that less than 1% of the population paid for all the election advertising we all had to endure. And that fraction of 1% will be amply rewarded by the politicians. The average voter gets that, and is pissed about it.

Both parties are playing the money game, and both have been corrupted by that game. Both are dutifully servicing the lobbyists and their donors. Neither is working for the general public. The average voter gets that. It's the single biggest reason why virtually all voters hate both parties with a passion. It's the single biggest reason why most have to hold their noses while voting and choose between the lesser of evils.

If the pundits are looking for fodder, there *are* serious questions that need answering. Where is authentic political leadership going to come from in our country? When and how is at least one of the major parties going to reconnect in a meaningful and enduring way with a disgusted and increasingly cynical citizenry? Is the public capable of imagining civic innovation to create a residence for the politically homeless if there is no admission of infidelity forthcoming from the Republicans or Democrats and no sincere attempt to patch things up with estranged voters?

Here's one more question in urgent need of an answer: How do we get beyond partisan gridlock and political paralysis so the many seemingly intractable problems plaguing our society can be tackled and solved? There always have been divisions and competing factions in America, and there always will be. But the political process used to serve the useful purpose of working out those differences so we could be governed. Today it actually magnifies our differences and aggravates the divisions.

Until we work our way through that conundrum it would be foolish to expect the electorate to do anything but continue to lurch, changing colors like a chameleon from election to election.

Problem is, there's a conundrum underneath that conundrum. We have a two-party system. America does not have a parliamentary democracy. We do not have coalition governments formed out of competing factions. We do not have proportional representation where those sitting in Congress or in our state legislatures are put there by voters in proportion to their share of the vote.[4] We do not have choice voting where voters are able to rank all candidates in order of preference.[5] We have winner-take-all elections. And we have a system that both favors and enforces the supremacy of two major parties. That system is full of legal, procedural and practical barriers to the organization and operation of a successful third party.

So here we are, stuck. Both parties are failing us. One party is seen as standing for big government, the other for little or no government. One is called conservative but is deeply dissatisfied with the status quo and seems hell-bent on returning America to the nineteenth century. The other is called liberal or progressive but in truth is the nation's true conservative party at the moment, dedicated merely to preserving advances it made decades ago when it had the gall to desire a New Deal or Great Society. In any case, today neither party is seen as truly working for the people. Both are seen as captive parties that owe allegiance to their big donors and ceaselessly cater to those wealthy interests.

We have one party that is scary and another that is scared. The choice for voters is an unpalatable one, when one's ambitions are both overly extreme and too backward for most people's tastes, and the other is paralyzed and afraid to lead. Just because voters do ultimately have to choose between the two doesn't mean they hold either in high esteem or fail to see their faults. The truth is most people hate both parties, as evidenced by the fact discussed in chapter 3 that more Americans do not feel comfortable identifying with either major party than at any time in the last three-quarters of a century. The ranks of the politically homeless are growing and growing fast.

The political class, on the other hand, is full of people who believe that perception is reality, and who are committed to spinning people dizzy so their distorted perception becomes a disfigured reality that favors the spinners and the benefactors on whose behalf they do their voodoo.

One party says government is not the solution but the problem. By word, it is against most everything government has done and proposes doing. By deed, it was responsible for the biggest expansion of government in the last 50 years. That inconvenient truth is the sprawling bureaucracy known as the Department of Homeland Security. DHS was created by the Homeland Security Act of 2002, which was sponsored by one of the anti-government party's top congressional leaders with co-sponsorship by well over 100 of that party's members before being overwhelmingly approved by both houses of Congress and signed into law by the anti-government party's president. A mere decade after its establishment, DHS ranks as the third largest cabinet-level federal agency.

This vast expansion of government power manifests itself in countless ways, from pat downs and full-torso scans to body cavity searches and phone wiretaps. It is the police state on steroids, courtesy of America's anti-government party.

Perception is not reality. Reality is reality. Unless we're too disoriented to see it.

The other party's devotees fancy themselves as working class heroes. But what Wisconsin Democrats did when major benefactors of theirs—the public employee unions—were under siege is not what they did when the housing bubble burst and foreclosures exploded and large numbers of people were losing their homes. What they did for public sector unions is not what they did for working class people caught in a financial vise when banks and Wall Street investment firms started behaving more like casinos and brought the economy to its knees. No walkouts. No mass demonstrations. No banksters sent to jail.

Democrats largely looked the other way at credit default swaps and collateralized debt obligations and hedge funds and derivatives and subprime mortgages and other such snake oil. Might that have had something to do with the fact that you see Goldman Sachs second and JP Morgan Chase sixth and Citigroup seventh on the list of biggest donors to the 2008 campaign of the party's national standard bearer?[6]

When public sector unions yelled jump, Democrats asked how high. In Wisconsin, Democratic senators fled the state and holed up across the border in Illinois for weeks to deny Republicans the needed quorum to hold votes on their union busting plan targeting most public employee bargaining units. But when hundreds of thousands of Americans without strong union representation were losing their private-sector jobs to outsourcing and offshoring, Democrats organized no meaningful opposition. They didn't flee the House and Senate chambers to deny Republicans a quorum and throw up an obstacle to congressional approval of "free trade" hoaxes like NAFTA and CAFTA. Hell, they helped pass those job-killing schemes.

If you listen carefully you hear a few platitudes and a little bellyaching from Democrats when Republicans double down on policies that haven't helped the economy but have hurt the poor and middle class for over 30 years and pass a new batch of tax cuts for the rich or a new round of deregulation allowing the air to be more easily polluted or the water more easily poisoned. But you don't see 100,000 people circling the Capitol. You don't see every parliamentary trick in the book being employed to throw a monkey wrench in the works.

Perception is not reality. Reality is reality. And most Americans are not too disoriented to see it. They can read the handwriting on the wall. What the writing says frustrates people to no end. Adding to the frustration is the seeming lack of alternatives to the rock and hard place the two major parties represent today.

Voting for a third-party or independent candidate may feel good, but as a practical matter it only can produce one of two results, neither of them good. Either it is a wasted vote or a spoiler vote. Four times Ralph Nader ran for president, twice as the Green Party's nominee and twice as an independent. Three times his candidacy's impact was inconsequential as he failed to win even 1% of the vote. But in 2000, Nader drew nearly 3 million votes or close to 3% of the total. Once a respected public interest lawyer and consumer rights hero, Nader became reviled by many on the left, blamed for siphoning precious votes away from Al Gore and putting George W. Bush in the White House.

Shortly before Nader made his quests, there were the 1992 and 1996 presidential campaigns of Texas oilman Ross Perot. Perot had a lot more money than Nader and used it to air lengthy infomercials and travel the country campaigning as an independent alternative to the major party nominees. He won more votes than Nader, too, but still fell far short of winning the election. In 1992, he captured nearly 19% of the popular vote and some of his Republican-leaning supporters and GOP establishment figures like Vice President Dan Quayle blamed him for siphoning votes away from President Bush and putting Bill Clinton in the White House, although post-election analyses showed he took votes away more or less equally from both Clinton and Bush.[7] Before the 1996 election, Perot formed the Reform Party of the United States and launched another third-party bid for the presidency. He only pulled about 8% of the vote on his second try.

In Wisconsin, the colorful brother of popular four-term Governor Tommy Thompson ran for the state's highest office in 2002 as a Libertarian. Once so broke that he ate his dog's biscuits, Ed Thompson went on to become a successful restaurateur and an elected mayor before launching his bid for governor. He made the strongest third-party showing Wisconsin had seen in nearly 60 years, garnering 10% of the vote. The votes he won came at the expense of the incumbent Republican governor, Scott McCallum. The candidate whose views least mirrored Ed Thompson's, Democrat Jim Doyle, won the office with just 45% of the vote. While his brother Tommy parlayed his long tenure as governor into a cabinet position in the Bush administration, Ed never advanced beyond being a small town mayor and never really lived down his role in putting a Democrat in the governor's office.[8]

The most successful third-party politician in recent memory has to be Minnesota's Jesse Ventura. The former professional wrestler—who performed as "The Body"—shocked the state's political establishment by winning the governorship in 1998 as the nominee of the Reform Party. But he struggled to govern as legislators from the two major parties obstructed him at every turn. He was gone after one term without much to show for it.

Most voters in America know how The Body must have felt when he left office. After all, so many among us cast ballots in election after election without much to show for it.

Not too long ago I went with my family to a science fair on the University of Wisconsin campus. There was everything from a way-over-my-head display on stem cell research to a crash-dummy demonstration of how much force is behind those highlight-reel hits by football players, which not coincidentally was next to a multimedia presentation on concussion research. Among the highlights of the fair was a Bill Nye the Science Guy type of show put on by Lebanese-born chemistry professor Bassam Shakhashiri featuring lots of explosions and other neat tricks.

At one point, Dr. Shakhashiri called attention to several long cylinders containing liquids of different colors. Before making them erupt like volcanoes, he pointed to each one and asked the audience what color the liquid was. For the first, quite a few shouted "blue." When he pointed to another, children and adults alike called out "red." He pointed to another containing what looked like water and asked again for his audience to identify the color. I mouthed the word "clear," and probably a dozen others gave the same answer out loud.

Professor Shakhashiri scolded us, noting that all of the liquids were clear but this last one was also colorless and further admonished us that clear and colorless are not the same thing. I learned that weekend what I should have already known, but for my own lackluster effort that earned only a C in high school chemistry.

Just as there is a difference between clear and colorless, there is a difference between freedom and democracy. We live in what unquestionably qualifies as a free and open society. There are undeniably some troubling assaults on essential liberties that must be beaten back, but overall we enjoy a great deal of social and economic freedom, especially when compared to most of the rest of the world.

At the same time, our democracy is quite ill. In a healthy democracy, political power is widely shared. Today in America, real power is concentrated in the hands of a very few. Most people believe their voices aren't being heard and a great many are convinced their votes don't count for much.

This is the American paradox. We are both free and increasingly undemocratic. We can more or less do as we please, but we have little or no say over anything important.

This is the genius of America's ruling class. They avoid the pitfalls that regularly ensnare two-bit dictators and authoritarian regimes by allowing us substantial freedom while still exercising near-full control over the direction of public debate and public policy. They do it by owning the information and systematically propagandizing the population. And they do it by working us and entertaining us to death, keeping us free but perpetually distracted while they go about accomplishing their aims. Those aims cost us a great deal, but we either don't notice or don't care because we freely occupy ourselves with an anesthetic combination of work-a-day responsibilities and trivial pursuits.

An open society is precious. Freedom is worth paying a steep price to have. But so is democracy. Trouble is, many if not most among us aren't worrying too much about democracy's sickly condition because we don't distinguish between the freedom we have and the healthy democracy we don't.

CHAPTER 7
THINKING VERTICALLY

There comes a time when politics stops making sense.

For my entire life and for generations before that, we've had two primary political factions in our country—Republicans and Democrats. And we've made sense of political debates and elections and acts of governing by thinking about where all the participants and their ideas fit on an ideological spectrum that runs horizontally from right to left. Then we label them in a shorthand—liberal, conservative, moderate—for easy reference.

Trouble is, the old labels don't seem to fit like they used to. Record numbers of citizens no longer are willing to call themselves either Democrats or Republicans. Maybe it's just that average folks have had their hopes, dreams, worries and fears ignored by the political class for so long that they've grown hostile toward both sides. Something tells me there's more to it than that, though.

The conventional political shorthand is becoming illegible, and the horizontal ideological spectrum on which that shorthand is based is becoming increasingly irrelevant because it no longer is especially helpful in making sense out of modern political realities.

Whether we realize it or not, the political spectrum has been turned on its head. It is vertical, not horizontal. The definitive question in today's politics is not whether you are standing with those on the left, right or middle; it is whether you are with those on the top or bottom or somewhere in between.

To vividly illustrate how outdated the old horizontal spectrum has become, try placing the two major political parties on a vertical spectrum. Who are the Democrats and Republicans standing with? Who are they working for? Those on top or those on the bottom?

Both parties belong at or near the top because both are catering to wealthy special interests and neither major party is listening to ordinary people or reliably acting on their behalf. The masses know who owns the politicians and our government, and it's not us. It's the big campaign donors and the lobbyists and the wealthy elites those lobbyists represent.

Every time the salt-of-the-earth Texas populist Jim Hightower is asked if it's time for a third party, he quips that he'd gladly settle for two. The old horizontal spectrum continues to foster the illusion of two parties with separate and distinct masters, while a vertical spectrum does a much better job of depicting how the two have really morphed into one in many ways.

Now think of where you and some of your family, friends and neighbors fit on the conventional left-to-right political spectrum. On the old horizontal spectrum, if you are like many if not most Americans, chances are you share common ground with some and have very little in common with many others, leaving you to think twice about sharing political views at social gatherings. But if you think vertically, it's a pretty sure bet that you and your acquaintances are at or near the same spot. We are boxed in by the horizontal rule. It not only creates illusions about the political establishment, it needlessly divides the rest of us by magnifying our differences and glossing over our commonalities.

Take two men, one poor and black, the other poor and white. The poor black lives in inner-city Milwaukee, the poor white in rural Clark County. Put them on the horizontal political spectrum. The poor black almost certainly is on the left. The poor white is more than likely somewhere right of center. The two are divided and politically conquered. Now flip the spectrum on its end, with those on stilts on the top and those in boots—you know, the kind with straps for pulling yourself up—on the bottom. Those two men suddenly are in the same spot.

Take two women, one a young schoolteacher, the other a clerical worker in her late 40s. The beginning teacher is making high 20s or low 30s. The middle-age office assistant is making roughly the same. The younger woman is a lapsed Catholic, the older one a churchgoing born again Christian. Try putting them on the horizontal spectrum. Chances are the teacher falls left of center and the clerk is on the right. Think vertically and the two fall in about the same place.

You get the picture. Thinking vertically not only has the potential to unite those who are currently divided, but also empower those who are presently conquered.

If we modernize the ideological spectrum and stop thinking right and left and start thinking up and down to make better sense of politics, we'll also be forced to update our political vocabulary. We'll no longer talk about liberals and conservatives and left wings and right wings. We'll need new shorthand, new labels. Then and only then will our speech again have a ring of truth when we tell each other who's on our side and who's not.

Such recalibration of political language will not come from the political class. That crowd is obsessed with who's right and who's left. Which is why they are so hopelessly out of touch with average citizens. As noted in chapter 3, if they'd spend half as much time thinking about what's right and wrong, we wouldn't be in the mess we're in. Maybe the public's regard for politicians wouldn't be somewhere between that of used car salesmen and child molesters.

Today's political labels have outlived their usefulness. Tags like "liberal" and "conservative" or "left" and "right" are supposed to help us make sense of the political world. The code is all garbled.

The word liberal comes from the Latin *liber*, which means "free." One dictionary defines liberal as "generous" and "tolerant; broad-minded" and "one who favors reform or progress."

President John F. Kennedy wrote in his book *Profiles in Courage*: "If by a 'Liberal' they mean someone who looks ahead and not behind, someone who welcomes new ideas without rigid reactions, someone who cares about the welfare of the people—their health, their housing, their schools, their jobs, their civil rights and their civil liberties—someone who believes we can break through the stalemate and suspicions that grip us in our policies abroad, if that is what they mean by a 'Liberal,' then I'm proud to say I'm a 'Liberal.' "[1]

Today most people who would fit these definitions fear the L word. It has become a loaded term. It has taken on new meanings, ones that make liberal people squirm. They now prefer to call themselves progressives. That too is a loaded term. It no longer means what it once did. The original Progressives were Republicans. And eventually there were Progressive Democrats as well as Progressive Republicans. Today, the word is understood by most to mean leftist and by quite a few as another word for Democrat.

If the dictionary is to be believed, liberals play offense and conservatives presumably then play defense. Indeed, among the dictionary definitions of conservative is "tending to preserve established institutions; opposed to change" and "moderate; cautious." Yet in modern politics, it's the self-described "conservatives" who are on the attack, seeking to dismantle New Deal and Great Society programs and do away with the social safety net, which they describe as more of a "hammock."[2] It's the "liberals" who always seem to be on their heels, seemingly incapable of an original thought, gamely defending decades-old programs.

George Will used to be fond of saying that conservatives are happy because the world is just as it should be. Indeed, if you look at Webster's definition of conservative, it speaks to the impulse to keep things the way they are.[3]

What neither Will nor Webster acknowledges is why true conservatives are so fond of the status quo, but it's obvious enough. The privileged like continuity. When social, political and economic conditions favor you, why change things?

Now consider Glenn Grothman, a West Bend, Wisconsin Republican who defeated the Senate Republican leader in a primary and went on to become assistant GOP leader in the upper house himself. Grothman calls himself a conservative. Most all political observers regard him as one. But he clearly doesn't fit the dictionary's definition, or Will's. He is most certainly not happy with the world just as it is. He favors a world that no longer exists.

Nicknamed "Spooky" by some of his own colleagues,[4] Grothman fears for the future of Christmas, and has waged an ongoing battle against holiday alternatives like Kwanzaa.[5] Today's social order clearly has him spooked. Men are no longer the sole breadwinners for families, and they no longer are the heads of households, a reality Grothman regularly rails against and tries his level best to legislate away. Women no longer are expected to be submissive to their husbands, barefoot and pregnant, tending hearth and home. Gays and lesbians don't have to stay in the closet. Blacks aren't required to sit on the back of the bus anymore.

Many in and around the Capitol dismiss Glenn Grothman as a kook. But what they fail to realize or at least acknowledge is that Grothman is now mainstream within today's Republican Party. He holds a key leadership position within his party in my state. There are hundreds if not thousands of Glenn Grothmans serving in public offices across America.

They carry the conservative label, but they are not conservatives. They are not happy because the world is just as it should be. They do not wish to keep things exactly as they are. They want less religious diversity; they want Christmas and only Christmas. They want "traditional" marriage and "traditional" families, with one man and one submissive woman. They want white people to hold most of the political power and most of the nation's wealth.

They realize the world is less and less what they long for it to be. They want to turn back the clock. Doing so is not a conservative act. It is retrogressive.

Glenn Grothman's party has a growing problem. More and more every day, our country is becoming less white, less male-dominated, less Christian, less "traditional." More and more every day, the reach of the GOP's appeal is thus narrowed. Today it is the party of angry white men. Spooked, middle-age or older, white men. Men like Glenn Grothman. It has lost the support of most women. It also doesn't have the support of most nonwhite people. It's having a hard time with our nation's youth.

That's why Republicans are continually expanding their war on voting and seeking new ways to effectively rig elections in their favor. Their political fortunes—and their hopes for social retrogression—rest on making it harder for certain "untraditional" classes of voters to have a say in the future.

Over the long haul, it is a losing battle. If Glenn Grothman truly represents West Bend, the city might want to consider changing its name to Last Gasp.

Even Grothman's base has its doubts. A local Rotary Club not far from the senator's home invited me to speak at an autumn lunch meeting. With an election right around the corner I engaged the audience—which was all-white, virtually all-male and all devoted to private enterprise—on the subject of election spending in general and all the repugnant campaign advertising in particular. I told them I could think of no other industry that would risk advertising this way. Can you imagine airlines advertising the way politicians do? No one in America would fly.

As I stood at the podium, over my left shoulder was a banner bearing Rotary's "Four-Way Test." Is it the TRUTH? Is it FAIR to all concerned? Will it build GOODWILL and BETTER FRIENDSHIPS? Will it be BENEFICIAL to all concerned? The club president was struck by how miserably campaign ads fail the test all four ways, and said so. Judging from the audience's reaction, he was speaking for the group, to be sure. I told them today's politicians don't fare any better on the test after they are elected and turn to governing.

That day I also shared with these merchants and brokers and entrepreneurs a five-way test of my own and applied it to today's major parties.

Are the parties of, by and for COMMON FOLKS? Not hardly. A royalty has taken over American politics and lords over both parties. Commoners are politically homeless.

Do they demonstrate COMMON DECENCY? Not by a long shot. Both sides seek power through campaign advertising that almost always is misleading and deceptive and often is downright untruthful. It is fantasy to believe power sought dishonestly will lead to decency in governing.

Do they use COMMON SENSE? Rarely if ever. One prime example is the national debt, where one party says cut social programs but increase spending on defense and keep cutting taxes for the wealthy, while the other puts social programs off limits, won't cut defense much but is willing to increase what the super-wealthy pay in taxes. Neither's math adds up to anything close to a balanced budget.

Do they find COMMON GROUND? Um, no. They are polarized to the point of dysfunction. The extremists among them regard compromise as a profanity. Moderates are on the verge of extinction. Statesmanship has become an alien concept. The use of wedge issues to divide us has been raised to an art form.

Are they working for the COMMON GOOD? Another failing grade. Time and again government policies are skewed to benefit the few at the expense of the many. The gap between the rich and the rest keeps growing. Economic inequality in America is reaching historic proportions.

Despite today's intensified inequities, the people of Wisconsin and America are not as hopelessly divided as the political pundits like to claim. A great many of us have a great deal in common. But the party bosses thrive on playing up what distinguishes them from their political enemies, and this leads them to ceaselessly drive wedges between groups of citizens.

There's much that needs doing if we are to restore some common sense and common decency to politics. Our endeavors need to start with the basics. We need new ways to talk about politics. We are sorely in need of some new labels. The old code fails us. Under a new lexicon, we could stop thinking from left to right and start thinking up and down. If the defining standard became whether you are for those on top or for those on the bottom, many "liberals" and "conservatives" fall in the same category as they slavishly service their wealthy campaign donors. The bankruptcy and obsolescence of the old labels become apparent.

There's significance in the increasing uselessness of our old political vocabulary. It means the ground has moved beneath us, but our language has not yet caught up to this shift in the tectonic plates of our democracy. Something historic is happening, but we haven't figured out how to talk about it yet. Once we do, politics will begin to make more sense to more people again. That can only result in something good.

Maybe instead of continuing to apply labels like "liberal" and "conservative" that are increasingly meaningless, we will begin talking about royals and commoners. Or stilts and boots. Possibilities abound. When we do, we will be accused of engaging in class warfare. And the accusations will come from the field generals in America's class wars, the very souls who have done the most to create historic disparities in income and wealth in our country. Just as the crookedest politicians go to the greatest lengths to manufacture suspicion about the ethical conduct of their opponents.

Once a political vocabulary suited to our times emerges, attention needs to turn to creating a political home for common folks. We need a common party. One where talk of the common good is not so uncommon.

For the record, I am not talking about creating a third party. I am talking about having at least one that truly owes its allegiance to the people.

CHAPTER 8
FROM THIRD TO FIRST

Clearly the current political landscape is stomach turning for most if not nearly all citizens. As previously noted, the number of Americans who can't bring themselves to embrace either major party is at its highest level in three-quarters of a century. Not much more needs to be said about the disillusionment so many feel about politics and those in power.

The question is what to do about it. Neither major party is seen as working for the common good or doing what's best for America. They are seen as working for the narrow, wealthy interests that fund them. This leads more than a few to pine for a third way.

But as was also earlier discussed, third parties in this country are destined to fail. Third parties fail because, well, their aim is to make it so we have three parties. For better or worse, ours is a two-party system. It is not a parliamentary democracy.

Third-party movements also routinely fail because they organize to the left of the Democrats or to the right of the Republicans (there's that horizontal thinking again!). Thus they largely operate on the political fringes, and only meaningfully compete for the votes of a small part of the electorate.

Third-party aficionados rightly lament that their fate is sealed by the fact that we have winner-take-all elections. They have a point when they say that if we had proportional representation or rank-order voting or one of its variants, things would be different.

Such reforms would improve our democracy and greatly benefit society. My group, the Wisconsin Democracy Campaign, and many others have advocated this kind of reform for years. But how do you get from point A to point B? How do you get a legislature controlled by the major parties to pass such reforms and then an executive from one of the major parties to sign them into law? The major parties would have to agree to weaken themselves and threaten their grip on power. Not bloody likely.

So the rules are rigged against third parties and changing the rules won't happen without the consent of the two major parties. How then do you loosen their stranglehold?

An answer can be found in the history books. Attempts to create alternatives that can shake the major parties to their foundations have succeeded at least twice—and both times they started in Wisconsin. In each case they were what I would call first-party movements, not third-party movements.

First-party movements do not aim to give us three parties. They force one of the two existing major parties to either adapt or perish. One time a major party got replaced. The other time both major parties were reformed.

In the time of slavery, the Whig Party was one of the two major parties in America. The Republican Party was born in 1854 in a one-room schoolhouse in Ripon, Wisconsin out of frustration over the lack of a true anti-slavery party and eventually drove the Whigs to extinction.[1] America's system returned the political arrangement to two major parties, with the upstart Republican Party replacing the too-stubborn-to-evolve Whigs. What happened those many years ago continues to echo today. The man who represented Ripon in Congress for 35 years, Republican Tom Petri, reminded delegates to his party's 2014 state convention of this history. Emphasizing what he called the Whig Party's "dysfunction" and the abundance of other fringe parties at the time, Petri said: "Ultimately, members of the dying political parties realized they could not succeed independently. They needed a coalition and a reinvention."

In reporting Petri's remarks, the *Wisconsin State Journal* underscored his characterization of events: "That's what happened in Ripon in 1854: The party's founders entered a little white schoolhouse as Whigs, Free Soilers, Abolitionists and Democrats, but came out as Republicans."[2]

The newspaper acknowledged the modern-day irony, noting that "Petri was a stark reminder of the struggle for the GOP's soul." The congressman's convention speech was a farewell address. Weeks earlier, he had announced he was leaving Congress rather than face a primary challenge from state Senator Glenn Grothman—remember "Spooky"?—who thinks Petri unacceptably centrist. Whether the GOP's future belongs to the likes of Glenn Grothman or Tom Petri remains to be seen. History establishes that the 1850s political reinvention of which Petri spoke endured for decades, helping to guide the nation through the Civil War and subsequent Reconstruction. Then out of the cauldron of bank failures and economic depression in the 1890s, the Progressive movement rose to challenge the Republicans and Democrats. Its genesis also traces to Wisconsin. In fact, it can be traced to a particular encounter that occurred on September 17, 1891, when Republican leader Philetus Sawyer offered a 35-year-old attorney named Robert M. La Follette a bribe to fix a court case. Furious, La Follette refused Sawyer's overture, later saying: "Nothing else ever came into my life that exerted such a powerful influence upon me." He proceeded to barnstorm the state speaking out against crooked politicians and corrupt timber and railroad barons. Those who followed La Follette called themselves "Progressive" Republicans. They believed that "the business of government was not business, but service to the common people."[3]

That first-party movement didn't end up replacing either major party, but reformed both. Both parties developed predominant Progressive wings. Teddy Roosevelt was elected president as a Progressive Republican. Soon after, Woodrow Wilson won the presidency as a Progressive Democrat. The nation's character, and Wisconsin's in particular, were fundamentally reshaped.

The lesson from the history books is to stop hoping for three parties and start focusing on creating one that is worth a damn. You do that by creating some competition in the form of a new political brand and then go to battle in major party primaries to win voters over to that new brand.

To be both constructive and successful, the brand can't be an appeal to the fringes. It has to be a threat to the major parties by strongly appealing to the heart of the electorate. Put another way, it can't seek to clip a party's wing, it has to cut out its heart. It also can't be a resurrection of an old political brand. The Progressive label, for example, doesn't mean what it once did; the term is now loaded with modern connotations. If there's a new political brand to be created, it needs a new name.

Rather than trying to run candidates on a separate party line on the ballot, leaving them vulnerable to the spoiler and wasted-vote phenomena, a first-party challenge aims to compete directly with the major parties in their own primary elections. Most people who end up voting for Republicans or Democrats are actually politically homeless. Most hate both parties. Create some competition within each party. Give people an appealing new option within each party.

In private industry, if a product is out there and no longer seems to meet the needs of consumers, some competitor jumps into the market with a new and improved product. The same principle needs to be applied to politics, in a realistic way that takes into account the way the American system is structured.

Third-party organizing has been tried many times, and many times it has failed. First-party organizing twice sprung up in Wisconsin out of frustration with the political establishment—when enough people were feeling alienated and politically homeless—and two times it succeeded in producing major political realignment and reform nationally. It is not hard to imagine that we are approaching another such moment when the established political arrangement can be subverted from within.

It certainly was not difficult for the billionaire brothers Charles and David Koch to see a time ripe for political subversion approaching. They planned the Tea Party movement for a decade before it burst on the American political scene.[4] What is perhaps most striking about the Tea Party is its grassroots appearances when it is made strictly of AstroTurf.[5] That it was designed to advance the interests of the Koch brothers is well established. Less noticeable than the Tea Party's inauthenticity but maybe even more significant is that, its name notwithstanding, the Kochs did not create a third party. They established a new political brand, and then used that invention to take over the Republican Party and turn it into an even more loyal servant and even more enthusiastic promoter of Koch Industries' agenda. They have to be pleased with the results of their efforts. Citizens need to understand what these two corporate tycoons clearly understand. If first-party organizing can be done to serve the narrow purposes of the Kochs to divide and conquer the rest of us for their own further enrichment, it can be done by regular citizens to make government a more faithful instrument of the people. The tactic works. It worked in the 1850s and again in the 1890s, when it was used to unite a divided nation and revitalize our republic. It is working now for the Koch brothers, but to a divisive and selfish end. Can we not imagine a more constructive and public-spirited purpose for this time-tested strategy?

Once the light bulb goes on for enough of us as it has for the Kochs, our success in harnessing the power of first-party thinking will hinge on our ability to get over a couple of humps. The first is the natural tendency to conclude that citizens cannot do what the Kochs have done because we lack their immense wealth. Remember, the first-party strategy was successfully employed by common folks in the nineteenth century, enabling them to break the stranglehold of their era's equivalents of the Koch brothers. And remember also that the Kochs understood that their money would be wasted on an attempt to establish a third party. They wisely focused on commandeering one of the existing parties.

The second hump we have to get over is the mindset of being divided. I repeat: The people of Wisconsin and America are not as hopelessly divided as the political pundits like to claim. A great many of us have a great deal in common. Many if not most in our society want a limited government. Limited not only in how much it takes from our pocketbooks, but also limited in other respects. Government has no place in the bedroom and its role should be limited to nonexistent in the doctor's office or at the death bed. Common threads abound that today's polarized politicians cannot see. Today both major parties are tools of the powerful and privileged. Neither is seen as working for the benefit of our whole country, and that perception in squarely rooted in the reality that neither party is working in such a fashion. Many if not most in our society clearly don't want government to do too much. But whatever the government does needs to be done for the benefit of all, not just an elevated few. There's another common thread right there.

Which party will see the common threads and begin using them to knit us back together is an open question. An even bigger question is what transformational force will compel them to open their eyes.

The genius of those who gathered in the little white schoolhouse in 1854 was their understanding of the power found in calling themselves something other than a Democrat or a Whig and uniting around a common creed. The better part of 40 years later, when that new creation had become encrusted with corruption, a young lawyer again brought about renewal by renouncing his party's brand and inventing a new political identity.

History has a way of repeating itself. Conditions have again grown ripe. Despite the political establishment's best efforts to convince us how divided we are, it is possible to imagine a shared creed. Today's commoners share an understanding that the biggest problem facing America in our time is a political system that caters to a few at the expense of the many. At the root of this problem is political corruption—a pervasive, systemic corruption that plagues us with "leaders" who are not free to lead and leaves our country paralyzed when it comes to dealing with the most challenging issues of our time.

Most Americans can see that both major political parties are failing America. Most understand the way politicians seek public office in this day and age—with advertising that is routinely misleading and often downright untruthful—is immoral and destructive to civic life. Power sought through dishonest means cannot possibly lead to just and honest policymaking or clean and open government.

Americans believe in hard work and self sufficiency. We also believe in looking out for the welfare of others. We believe in a free market, not a market manipulated to favor the most politically privileged participants in our economy. The vast majority of us would like to see one-for-all economics—policies ensuring that the fruits of a vibrant economy benefit the whole of society. We see the need for both rural revitalization and urban renewal. Instead of subsidizing global conglomerates, efforts to stimulate the economy should emphasize community-based small enterprise development, empower local entrepreneurs and cooperatives, and enable us to once again grow together rather than grow apart. We believe supply-side economic theory has it wrong. Demand, not supply, is the primary driver of economic growth. Trickle-down policies have been a miserable failure, never producing more than a trickle for the masses and producing grotesque economic inequality and the slow but steady extermination of the middle class.

Most Americans understand that government is necessary to a civil and just society and prosperous economy, but insist on a limited government—one that is as small as possible and only as big as required to do what society needs done collectively. Government programs that work should be supported and ones that do not should be reformed or ended. Most importantly, what government does must serve the broad public interest and promote the common good, not just benefit those who lavishly fund election campaigns or have high-priced lobbyists advocating on their behalf.

We don't act like it, but most Americans can agree that it is wise to live within our means and pay for what we get today instead of mortgaging the future and saddling generations to come with our debts. We agree on the need for one-for-all taxation. We see no need for new taxes, but are in agreement that everyone should pay the ones we already have. There should be one tax system that applies equally and fairly to all, not two as is effectively the case today—one for the wealthy and well-connected, enabling them to avoid paying their fair share, and another for the rest of us without the tax shelters and escape hatches.

Most Americans can appreciate that we are all in the same boat and will sink or sail together. Most can see the sense in waging war on poverty rather than on poor people. We believe it is everyone's right to pursue material gain and accumulate wealth, but vigorously object to its use to buy government favors or special treatment.

Most Americans believe in aspiring to intelligence, not belittling it. Most see that becoming well educated and learning to think critically should be valued and expected, not feared or obstructed. Education is our best hope for building a better and more prosperous future, and our best weapon against economic and social decline. For our nation's youth to have a reasonable chance of experiencing the American Dream in the twenty-first century, higher education needs to be made as accessible and affordable in the future as primary and secondary education have been up to now.

Most Americans believe in science. And most understand we all have a duty to respect nature and take care of the air, water and land. Environmental protection is not the enemy of economic development. A healthy economy and healthy planet must go hand in hand. We can increasingly see that there are actually three bottom lines in business. A truly productive and successful company is one that is financially profitable, one whose workers and customers are treated justly and well, and one that is a responsible steward of natural resources.

Most Americans believe in the free exercise of religion. In the interest of safeguarding this freedom, most can appreciate the importance of the separation of church and state, as state intrusion into religious practice intolerably threatens the freedom to worship while church influence over governing poses a grave and unacceptable danger to democracy.

Most Americans value the right of privacy and place trust in individuals to make their own life choices and in families to serve as the moral backbone of our society. The limited government we insist on should not only be restrained in matters of the economy, it should be unintrusive with respect to our personal lives, morality and sexuality.

Most Americans believe in standing for and working to guarantee and preserve the basic human rights of all people regardless of race, gender, class, physical condition or sexual orientation.

Most Americans have all these things in common, and most also share the feeling of being politically homeless. Most are ready for a new brand of politics, just as the abolitionists who gathered in Ripon in 1854 were ready and that young lawyer was ready in 1891.

It is time to imagine a new political identity.

CHAPTER 9
BRANDS, BREEDS AND SUBVERSIVE DEEDS

The biggest threat to the ruling class is a long memory. You remember what was, you imagine what can be.

As spelled out on these pages, we have once again been visited by conditions eerily reminiscent of those known by the young lawyer who came to be known as "Fighting Bob." We again encounter a challenge like the one faced by the people who banded together in the schoolhouse in Ripon. The actions taken then and the progress they produced are known to those familiar with these slices of history. As was the case so long ago, the need for imagination that yields political renewal is self-evident in our day.

But when you remember when and how the donkey became the symbol of the Democrats and the elephant the emblem of the Republicans, you realize that no one has dared to imagine for a very long time when it comes to political brands.

The donkey's association with the Democrats dates all the way back to 1828. During Andrew Jackson's presidential campaign his opponents called him a jackass, which amused Jackson and inspired him to use the image of the strong-willed animal on his campaign posters. Later, cartoonist Thomas Nast used the Democratic donkey in newspaper cartoons and made the symbol famous.

Turns out Nast also had a hand in enshrining the Republican elephant. In an 1874 cartoon, Nast drew a donkey clothed in lion's skin, scaring away all the animals at the zoo. One of those animals, the elephant, was labeled "The Republican Vote." That's all it took for the elephant to become the enduring symbol of the Republican Party.[1]

So here we are well into the twenty-first century and the logos of the two major political brands are nineteenth-century creations. What exactly are their relevance in this day and age? Donkeys are known to be stubborn, not especially bright, but possess great endurance. Another name for donkey is ass, perhaps the only thing about the animal that conjures up images of today's Democrats. Elephants are slow moving, powerful and are said to have long memories. They are a staple spectacle in American zoos, but otherwise have no meaningful place in American life and do not do a thing for the average American. Wait a minute, maybe the elephant still is an apt symbol of the GOP.

We live in a moment where we have increasingly despised political parties and, perhaps fittingly, those parties are represented by increasingly irrelevant and even comical symbols. We live in a moment that cries out for political innovation. We need a new breed of politician, and even more than that we need a new political household that offers living quarters to estranged citizens.

If a compelling case for a new political brand is building—and I think it is, what with the swelling ranks of the politically homeless and their utter dissatisfaction with both major parties—then what should it be?

A good symbol needs to be familiar, instantly recognizable and memorable. And, well, symbolic. It needs to be something that people from just about every walk of life and every part of America can relate to and identify with.

What if the politically homeless across the ideological spectrum could start to see their common plight, namely that a privileged few are indulging their wildest dreams at the many's expense? What if the disaffected took further notice that America doesn't have a parliamentary system but rather one that assiduously reinforces a two-party landscape? And what if that caused them to stop toying with the idea of joining a third party that only stakes out territory to the left of the Democrats or to the right of the Republicans? What if they also got tired enough of holding their noses while voting and choosing between the lesser of evils, tired enough to think seriously about creating a first-party insurgency aimed at either transforming or supplanting at least one of the major parties?

What twenty-first-century-appropriate symbol would be emblematic of American commoners and symbolize their shared political aspirations?

Blue jeans.

Most everyone wears them. Men wear them. Women wear them. Young and old alike wear them. Southerners wear them. So do northerners. They are in fashion on both coasts, and are popular in America's heartland. People of every race, color and creed wear them. Kids wear them to school. They are worn by construction workers and on the assembly line and factory floors. We wear them at home, and when we go shopping, and at church, and increasingly at the office—and not just on casual Fridays anymore.

If there is one thing today that every average American has in common with any other, it is blue jeans. What could better symbolize the political identity of the masses than blue jeans? What stands in starker contrast with the stuffed shirts in the boardrooms, the K Street lobbyists who do their bidding, and the suits on Capitol Hill whose pockets are lined?

What if enough of those masses were to reject both the elephant and the ass? What if they embraced a new brand, politically speaking? A symbol with the common touch and the fashion currency and comfort of blue jeans? Imagine this new brand catches on and then a few among the masses start challenging Republicans and Democrats alike in GOP and Democratic primary elections, running as Blue Jean Democrats and Blue Jean Republicans. It is enough to evoke memories of what happened in 1854 and again in 1891. And nothing is a greater threat to the ruling class than a long memory.

Any new brand will be aided by the damaged condition of the old brands. The Republican brand of less government and lower taxes is badly undercut by the reality discussed in chapter 6 that the party recently presided over the biggest expansion of the federal government in the last half a century. The takeover of the party by extremists spawned by the faux-grassroots Tea Party movement further harms the Republican brand. For their part, the Democrats' brand as the party of the less fortunate does not square with their uneven treatment of working class constituencies and their allergy to the issue of poverty. And the Democrats' status as the party of government at a time when the public's faith in government is nearly depleted leaves them with an especially damaged brand.

Symbolism matters. It serves as shorthand for volumes about values and vision. There has to be substance behind any new symbol. It needs to represent something real and valuable, a common creed and shared political platform like the ones people united around in 1854 and 1891, although a modern one like that described at the end of chapter 8. New branding needs to be accompanied by new thinking. Compelling alternatives to the policies of the old brands must be advanced.

There is no better place to start than with the single biggest problem that most politicians in both major parties are loathe to address, namely the fact that America used to grow together and now is growing apart, with obscene concentrations of income and wealth in the hands of a very few. As previously discussed, Democrats across the land have been unable to trademark an effective alternative to Republican supply-side theory, better known as "trickle-down economics." Instead they have indulged the impulse to duck and cover for fear of being called socialists. Leaders bearing any useful new brand will have to stand their ground. That ground is solid. America—which has never been socialist—once had economic policies under which the country grew together for the three decades after World War II. Every income class got ahead. In the three decades that followed, trickle-down became the economic law of the land and America's rich got vastly richer, the poor got poorer and more numerous, the middle class shrunk, and our nation's youth were sentenced to debt.

Perhaps no better controlled experiment on the validity of trickle-down theory can be found than the recent economic experience of my home state of Wisconsin and neighboring Minnesota. In so many ways, the two states are twins. Both share a common ethnic ancestry and cultural heritage; both were settled by Germans and other northern Europeans. Both have extreme climates, with brutal winters and summers where temperatures can reach triple digits. Minnesota calls itself the "Land of 10,000 Lakes." Wisconsin has considerably more than that, and Minnesota probably does too. Farming is important economically to both states and fundamental to the fabric of society in each place. Populist politics is part of that fabric: Wisconsin birthed the Progressive movement and Minnesota its own unique Democratic-Farmer-Labor Party.

In 2011 the twins started adorning themselves in very different clothes, so to speak. Wisconsin doubled down on trickle-down while Minnesota chose the opposite economic path. After Scott Walker's election as governor, he and his allies who gained control of the legislature mounted strident attacks on union organizing, engineered some of the deepest cuts to education anywhere in the nation,[2] and ushered in tax reductions skewed in favor of the wealthy.[3] Minnesota also had a new legislature and new governor in Mark Dayton, and they raised taxes by more than $2 billion but made the top 1% of earners pay nearly two-thirds of the new taxes. Most of the new revenue went to boost spending on K-12 and higher education as well as start new programs providing all-day kindergarten and greater

MIKE McCABE

access to early childhood education, making Minnesota one of the few states to raise education spending amidst the Great Recession.

Wisconsin refused to establish a state health insurance exchange or expand Medicaid, even though the federal government offered to cover all costs for three years and most costs after that. Minnesota expanded Medicaid to cover an additional 35,000 people and accepted Washington's offer to pick up the cost. Wisconsin's constitution bans gay marriage. Minnesota voted to embrace marriage equality.

Industrial titans insist Wisconsin's policies make for a more favorable business climate, and supply-side theorists steadfastly predict such policies will result in a more dynamic economy and produce more jobs. It isn't working out that way. With Walker at the helm, Wisconsin lagged behind Minnesota in job creation and economic growth. At a time when Minnesota had the fifth fastest growing state economy, Wisconsin ranked 34th for job growth. Forbes ranked Minnesota the eighth best place for business, while Wisconsin continued to rank in the bottom half of states.[4]

Neither state's economic policies qualify as socialism. But while Wisconsin feeds the rich and tries to manufacture supply, Minnesota stokes demand by spreading the wealth. Wisconsin went with tailored suits and Minnesota opted for blue jeans. Jeans made the stronger fashion statement, economically speaking.

It remains to be seen how many will remember how these two twins parted company after the Great Recession and where their paths led. The work of persuading multitudes—started by Reagan and Bush, extended by Clinton, intensified under the second Bush and sustained during the Obama years—that prosperity will trickle down from the mountaintops to irrigate vast plains and sprawling valleys depends on people forgetting. Remembering is subversive. There is no greater threat to the ruling class than memory.

CHAPTER 10
FINDING THE MISSING R

Inventing a new political identity and, more importantly, a new political household for American commoners are necessary for renewal of our ailing democracy, but are not sufficient. These steps must be followed by at least six others. The next six chapters are devoted to describing them.

First things first. As a people, we need to come to terms with the desecration of the First Amendment. This cherished possession of all Americans is a mere 45 words long, but a lot is packed into those 45 words. The First Amendment to the U.S. Constitution guarantees all of us five basic freedoms—the freedom of speech, freedom of religion, freedom of the press, the right to peaceably assemble, and the right to petition your government.

All five have endured beatings over the years. But it is the freedom of speech whose condition is most critical. The declining health of the right to speak has not come about overnight. For a great many Americans, however, a light bulb went on in 2010 when the Supreme Court dropped a bomb on the electoral landscape with its decision in *Citizens United v. Federal Election Commission* giving the nation's ultra-wealthy a virtual monopoly on political speech. That ruling has ignited something of a firestorm, with voters of every political stripe united in overwhelming opposition and a growing movement pushing nationwide for a constitutional amendment overturning the decision.[1] But the assault on the First Amendment did not start with *Citizens United*. And it does not end there.

As discussed in chapters 4 and 5, the Supreme Court radically reinterpreted the meaning of those 45 words starting in 1976. The First Amendment was already 185 years old when the nation's highest court, ruling in *Buckley v. Valeo*, equated money with speech. The word "money" does not appear among the 45 words, but the court effectively inserted it.

Money is many things, but it is not a synonym for speech. It is an asset or property. It is a measure of the value of goods or services. It is even a means of amplifying the volume of speech. But it is not speech itself.

Beginning in 1976, the commercialization of speech commenced in earnest and a central First Amendment right started to transform into a commodity. It ceased to be a right and started becoming a privilege that must be purchased at great expense.

In 2010 the court built on *Buckley* with its decision in *Citizens United v. FEC*, marrying two legal doctrines to draw the conclusion that corporations, unions and other interest groups can spend as much as they want to influence American elections. It is important to understand that the court did not rule there can be no limit on what the *people* who run corporations, unions and advocacy organizations spend to sway voters. The court decided the *things* themselves could not be restricted.

The legal theories that were wedded in *Citizens United* included the money-is-speech doctrine from *Buckley* and the idea that corporations are people, a proposition whose genesis can be traced back to an 1886 case, *Santa Clara County v. Southern Pacific Railroad*. That case involved a dispute over taxation of railroad property. In deciding the dispute, the justices did not rule that corporations are persons entitled to citizenship rights and equal protection under the law guaranteed by the Fourteenth Amendment. That conclusion was added by the court reporter, who wrote in a note attached to the decision that the justices all shared that opinion. Once *Santa Clara* was cited as precedent by future courts in subsequent cases, the legal doctrine of "corporate personhood" was established. The Bill of Rights and the Fourteenth Amendment were turned on their heads.[2]

Four years after handing down its decision in *Citizens United*, the court took another step toward dismantling legal protections against government corruption by striking down a key federal limit on political donations made directly to candidates, PACs and party committees in *McCutcheon v. FEC*. The ruling gave barely 1,200 donors nationally—0.000003% of the American population—vastly greater ability to influence elections with their money.[3]

Santa Clara, Buckley, Citizens United and *McCutcheon* taken together effectively remove the "r" from free speech. In the political arena, speech is anything but free. It is ridiculously expensive, what with the prohibitive price of TV air time and the other only-slightly-less-costly means of political communication. Only a privileged few with vast wealth are able to do much talking. If you are not a wealthy political donor, you still have a constitutionally protected right to speak. But you have little or no way to make your voice heard.

After the *Citizens United* ruling and a subsequent decision in a related case, *SpeechNow.org v. Federal Election Commission*, a new kind of political action committee known as a Super PAC was created in July 2010.[4] Their impact on federal elections has been enormous, not to mention grotesquely disfiguring to democracy. In the 2012 elections, 32 donors to Super PACs matched all of the money raised from small donors by President Obama and his rival Mitt Romney combined. Yep, you heard me right: the top 32 Super PAC donors—giving nearly $10 million apiece—contributed a total of $313 million to finance election advertising by these special interest committees. Obama and Romney received $313 million from roughly 3.7 million Americans who gave less than $200 each.[5]

MIKE McCABE

If the Supreme Court's logic is correct and money equals speech, then each of the 32 Super PAC donors spoke with 115,000 times the volume of each of the nearly 4 million people who gave much smaller amounts to the candidates. And remember, the U.S. population at the time was over 311 million. That means well over 300 million people gave nothing at all. They did not speak. Not even at a whisper. The mute button was on for them.

The one-percenters have cynically but brilliantly appealed to core American values to justify their redefinition of 45 of the most important words ever written and to effectively legalize political bribery again. Any attempt to limit the capacity of the rich and powerful to buy politicians and own our government was savaged as an attack on freedom and labeled "speech rationing." Any attempt to blunt the effects of big money's influence by providing small-dollar public financing to candidates was assailed as "welfare for politicians" and "socialized campaigning."

Clever. Orwellian as hell, but clever. You can have open, honest, corruption-free government, or you can have free speech, but not both. You can have unbought and un-bossed elected representatives, or you can keep the First Amendment.

These are false choices, and must be seen as such. We can have freedom *and* democracy. They are not the same thing, but neither are they mutually exclusive. We can guarantee all people the right to speak freely without at the same time granting them a license to buy off our elected representatives and corrupt our government.

Seeing through the false choices—and ultimately refusing to make them—starts with an understanding that no constitutional right is absolute or unconditional. Among other things, the First Amendment guarantees freedom of the press. But ask any of the countless journalists who have been jailed or the judges who put them behind bars if there are limits to that freedom.

Or take the Second Amendment. "A well regulated militia, being necessary to the security of a free state, the right of the people to keep and bear arms, shall not be infringed."

Put aside for a moment that some believe the "well regulated militia" clause means the Second Amendment bestows a collective right to bear arms, not an individual right. Most people, and most courts, believe it protects an individual's right to possess weapons. But that doesn't mean that individuals have an unconditional right to keep and bear *any and all* arms. For instance, no one in their right mind would say the Second Amendment establishes an individual's right to possess nuclear arms.

Just as an individual's possession of a weapon of mass destruction would pose an intolerable threat to other community members' rights to life, liberty and security, the First Amendment right of free speech likewise can be exercised by a few in a way that does violence to citizen rights and the common good.

We have reached that point in American politics.

Which is why it is time to start distinguishing between the exercise of First Amendment rights and the abuse of those rights. And why it is imperative that we restore the pre-1976 understanding of those 45 words and put the "r" back in free speech.

Lest we forget...

"I hope we shall... crush in its birth the aristocracy of our monied corporations which dare already to challenge our government to a trial of strength and bid defiance to the laws of our country."[6]

Ring a bell? Any idea who said it? It wasn't Marx or Lenin. Not Mao or Castro.

It was none other than the father of American republicanism, Thomas Jefferson.

Jefferson, like his revolutionary brethren, was deeply wary of corporate power. In order for the people to govern, he believed the "aristocracy of monied corporations" needed to be kept on a short leash, in the form of revocable charters that limited corporations to strictly commercial activities and required them to serve the public interest.

Jefferson famously articulated the need for a wall of separation between church and state. He less famously warned that if the people were to remain sovereign for long, a wall of separation between corporations and politics was essential.

That wall stood during the new nation's first century. As discussed, it came under assault in 1886, when a little-noticed note written by a clerk was added to a Supreme Court ruling and became the law of the land.

Americans typically are hard pressed to name more than a handful of Supreme Court decisions. Most everyone's heard of *Roe v. Wade*. And *Brown v. Board of Education*. But chances are pretty good you hadn't come across *Santa Clara County v. Southern Pacific Railroad Company* before now. It's certainly not taught in many high school history classes.

Santa Clara's accidental precedent dealt Jeffersonian democracy a severe blow by granting corporations the same rights as people under the Fourteenth Amendment. Said another way, the court re-wrote the constitution. The court rewrote it some more in *Buckley*. And a lot more in *Citizens United*.

But just as *Citizens United* was not the first or only act of judicial tampering with the plain meaning of the First Amendment, it is not solely responsible for the demolition of Jefferson's wall of separation. Wisconsin's Fighting Bob La Follette understood Jefferson's warning about a corporate aristocracy. In response to the political corruption of his day and the massive power of the timber and railroad barons, La Follette and his allies outlawed corporate contributions to political campaigns and corporate election spending more than a century ago.

La Follette's ban on corporate electioneering in Wisconsin held up for almost exactly 100 years. Then corporate interests began running so-called "issue ads." These ads looked and sounded just like campaign ads, but thanks to an obscure footnote in the 1976 ruling in *Buckley*, the ads' corporate sponsors were able to skirt campaign finance disclosure laws.

No disclosure, no evidence of corporate contributions. La Follette's ban was rendered meaningless overnight. A flood of corporate money has poured into Wisconsin politics ever since. As the floodwaters swamped Wisconsin, they washed over the rest of the country as well.

Citizens United is better known, but the eventual impact of *Santa Clara* probably qualifies it as the most profoundly anti-Jeffersonian court decision of all time. If not *Santa Clara*, then surely *Buckley*. It created a "magic words" test for campaign advertising that exempts interest groups from disclosure requirements if they avoid using words like "vote for," "vote against," "elect" or "defeat" in their ads. Never mind that almost no candidate- or party-sponsored ads contain such words, just as no soft drink ads are so uncool as to say "buy Pepsi" or "drink Coke." Later this loophole was further cemented in place by a 2007 ruling in *Federal Election Commission v. Wisconsin Right to Life*.[7] What *Citizens United* did three years later was to free corporations from the need to perform this phony charade. They now can spend unlimited sums to explicitly advocate the election or defeat of candidates.

Our country first shamefully embraced, then struggled mightily with, and ultimately exorcised a great anti-democratic demon—the repugnant notion that people can be property. But we have blithely accepted the similarly ridiculous supposition that property can be a person, and allowed it to be joined in matrimony with the contention that money is synonymous with speech. Our inattention to the gradual erosion of a core republican principle—that "we the people" and only "we the people" are sovereign—must haunt Jefferson in his grave. Far from crushing the aristocracy of monied corporations in its birth, as Jefferson exhorted us to do, the Supreme Court has been handing out crowns.

MIKE McCABE

Lest we forget…

"Unless the mass retains sufficient control over those entrusted with the powers of their government, these will be perverted to their own oppression, and to the perpetuation of wealth and power in the individuals and their families selected for the trust." Jefferson again.[8]

We have some walls to rebuild.

CHAPTER 11
SOME
HAND-HELD DEVICE

That Bill Proxmire could get elected in Wisconsin for over 30 years while spending as little as $145 to make his case to the voters was no accident. That Scott Walker had to spend more than $36 million decades later to barely survive an attempt to recall him from office in the same state also was no accident.

When Proxmire was running, newspapers were king in American politics. Most people got most of their information about politics and government and candidates and elections by reading the newspaper. Television was fast becoming a fixture in American life, but it was still in its infancy as a force in politics. It was not yet the primary means of political communication. Candidates did not pay for TV ads. There were no party fronts or shadowy interest groups airing thousands of 30-second doses of poison. Prox was a singularly gifted politician who had a knack for getting his name in the paper. He was a tireless face-to-face campaigner. His formula worked. He never lost an election for a seat in the United States Senate.

Today, Proxmire-style campaigns aren't possible, at least not at the state or national level and increasingly not even at the local level. In Wisconsin we've seen campaign spending in races for state assembly reach seven figures, state senate contests top eight figures, and elections for statewide offices like governor approach nine figures. What the hell happened in the span of little more than a single generation? TV happened.

It's not that TV didn't exist in the 1960s or 1970s. It obviously did. But it wasn't the primary way candidates for office reached potential voters. It is now. TV is king of American politics. The madness that is the modern campaign arms race in national and state elections has two fundamental causes. One is the reinterpretation of the First Amendment to equate money and speech, and the other is the high cost of buying air time on television. TV advertising is the biggest single expense in modern political campaigns, and that expense is staggering. In the 2012 presidential election alone, more than $1 billion was spent on TV ads.[1] On top of that, there were hundreds of congressional elections and thousands of state and local contests where hundreds of thousands of paid appeals aired on TV.

At the root of the problem is the fact that America is the world's only major democracy without some kind of system to supply free television air time to candidates for office.[2] Here, candidates have to pay—and pay dearly—to communicate with voters. When Supreme Court justices said money equals speech, they weren't kidding. Today, a candidate's campaign is little more than a glorified collection agency for the TV stations.

It won't always be this way. A time will come when television is no longer king of American politics, when TV is no longer the primary way most people learn about politics and elections and candidates for office. One day, some hand-held device that hasn't even been invented yet will be the primary means of political communication. That day is a ways off. At my age, I am not even certain I will live to see it. My son surely will.

When I say that, I am not denying the digital age is upon us. Nor am I downplaying the importance and ubiquitous presence of the Internet in our lives. The Internet is a big deal, but it is just now beginning to scratch the surface of its potential as a political instrument.

More and more campaign managers and political media buyers are investing in online advertising, but the buys are miniscule compared to the money still being poured into television. There is a reason for that. Political professionals know that television is where their candidates need to be in order to reach the maximum number of voters. The Internet will be king of American politics one day, but that day is not here yet. Not even close. TV still reigns supreme.

When the day comes and the Internet assumes the throne, campaigning for office could be revolutionized and democracy transformed, *if* we still have a free and open Internet. That's a big if.

As you read this, powerful forces in the telecommunications industry are working to refashion the rules governing our online experience and radically change the Internet as we know it today. There is an obvious profit motive driving their actions. But there also are political implications. If the third stage of ownership described in chapter 5 is to have a future, America's royals need to colonize the Internet as they have television. For it to become the exclusionary force in politics that they need it to become, Internet speech must become as prohibitively expensive in the future as televised speech is today.

We have become accustomed to a certain kind of experience when we log onto the Internet. Most of us take that experience for granted. Most of us are not as wary and vigilant as Free Press, the national advocacy group that tirelessly stands guard to protect Internet freedom. Most of us take as a given that we can access any website we want, whenever we want. We have a hard time imagining an Internet experience that does not permit users to do site searches, send emails and instant messages, watch online videos and listen to podcasts—at any time. We expect to be able to attach game controllers, wireless routers or other devices to enhance our online experience.

As the activists at Free Press keep trying to remind us, none of this is a given. What makes all this possible is something called "Network Neutrality," the operating principle of a free and open Internet. Net Neutrality means Internet service providers cannot discriminate between different kinds of Web content and applications. For example, when you use a search engine, you see a list of the sites that are the closest match to your request—not just those that paid the most to reach you. That is Net Neutrality at work.

Telecommunications giants want to get rid of Net Neutrality in the worst way. They want to be able to charge extra for prompt access to all websites, and for permission to plug in devices, and for the capacity to run applications. They want to be able to charge website operators, application providers and device manufacturers for the right to use the network. Those who don't pay the required premiums will find their sites won't load as quickly, and their applications and devices won't work as well. Without Net Neutrality, a network operator could slow down the website of a competitor so much that it's unusable, or block it altogether.

Network operators call their dream a "tiered" Internet. Today's Internet has been described as an information superhighway. Tomorrow's Internet could become a system of toll roads. Pay to get in the top tier and your site and your service will run fast. Pay less for a lower tier and you're stuck in the slow lane.

As noted, there is a profit motive for what amounts to double dipping. With the Internet we know now, network operators charge consumers for Web access. In the future they want to charge you initially for access to the network, and then charge you again and again for the things you do while you are online. There also is a profit motive for digital discrimination. The founding principle of the Internet was that every website, every feature and every service should be treated the same. Altering the anti-discrimination rules of Net Neutrality—or doing away with them altogether—not only would create an unrecognizable Internet experience, it also would stifle economic and social innovation. The level playing field of today's Internet is what enables bloggers to compete with Rupert Murdoch's media empire for readers. It is what empowers up-and-coming musicians to build underground audiences long before their songs crack the top 40. It is what spawns EBays and Amazons, and makes it possible for upstarts to compete with established retailers and big boxes for customers without facing insurmountable hurdles. With a pay-per-view Internet, inventors and entrepreneurs and their startups would be muscled out of the marketplace by big corporations that pay for a top spot on the Web.[3]

It is easy enough to see how network operators could amass even greater profits by dumping Net Neutrality, even as they unwisely but perhaps inadvertently hinder the next generation of inventors and innovators and thinkers and dreamers and anyone else who cannot afford top-tier online access.

Not much imagination is required to see how a tiered Internet also would shape our politics once television's supremacy wanes and the electoral impact of the digital age reaches full flower. The playing field would decidedly tilt in favor of big-money interests as their voices would enjoy a virtual online monopoly. Any citizen or any group without the means to buy top-tier service would be frozen out. Political innovation would be stifled.

All of which brings to mind the oft-told story of Benjamin Franklin being approached as he left the Constitutional Convention by citizens asking what sort of government the delegates had created. Franklin famously answered: "A republic, if you can keep it."[4]

In a free, open, non-discriminatory Internet, we have at our disposal a creation with inestimable potential to renew and reinvigorate that republic—if we can keep it.

CHAPTER 12
AND THAT'S THE WAY IT IS

Whether most Americans get most of their information about politics from television, as is the case today, or the Internet, as will be the case in the not-too-distant future, we need news. It is the lifeblood of democracy.

It is well established that there is a massive and growing gulf between the rich and the rest of us. In 2012, the top 10% of earners took half the income in our country and more than a fifth of U.S. income went to the top 1%—the highest share since the government began collecting the data a century ago.[1]

But America's information inequality is at least as pronounced as its economic inequality. A Pew Research Center study shows a widening gap between the information-rich and information-poor. America's dominant news source is television, and Pew sliced the TV news audience into thirds—heavy, medium and light viewers. Heavy viewers watch a little over two hours of TV news a day, medium viewers barely watch a quarter of an hour and light viewers average only two minutes a day. In other words, the top third of news consumers does 88% of the TV news viewing. The middle third accounts for 10%

of news consumption, and the bottom third accounts for just 2%. Online news consumption is no more democratic. More than a third of Americans spend an average of only 90 seconds a day getting news over the Internet.[2]

What this says is that America has an information underclass. And two-thirds of the population belongs to that underclass. Given what Pew is finding about the news consumption habits of young adults—not only that they read, see and hear far less news than their grandparents and parents, but also that they show no signs of an increasing appetite for news as they age—the chances are great that the information underclass will grow ever larger and become permanent.[3]

It is always tempting for older generations to lament the perceived irresponsibility of their kids, and what's happening to news consumption will no doubt prompt more hand-wringing. Many will heap blame on the younger generations for tuning out. Fewer will seriously contemplate the uncomfortable fact that younger Americans have some perfectly good reasons for turning off the news.

Listen to John Mayer's 2006 anthem of discontent with the nation's leaders and his generation's powerlessness, "Waiting on the World to Change,"[4] and it's hard to deny he had a point.

"When you trust your television, what you get is what you got; when they own the information, oh, they can bend it all they want."

Around the time Mayer wrote those lyrics, a top Fox News executive was explaining why he fired two reporters and the general manager of a Tampa, Florida Fox affiliate over their plans to air a story critical of chemical industry giant Monsanto, a major Fox advertiser. "We paid $3 billion for these television stations. We'll decide what the news is. The news is what we say it is."[5] And the head of the Clear Channel radio empire was similarly huffing and puffing: "We're not in the business of providing news and information. We're not in the business of providing well-researched music. We're simply in the business of selling our customers products."[6]

Maybe, just maybe, our nation's youth are not acting irresponsibly but rather are showing an admirable resistance to brainwashing. What is clear is that when searching for the truth about what is happening in our world, many are concluding they are better off looking for it on Comedy Central than on the news networks. It is a sad commentary on the current state of American journalism that so many believe fake news shows offer them more real news than news programs do.

A big part of the problem stems from increasing concentration of media ownership. In the early 1980s, 50 corporations controlled the vast majority of all news media in America. At the time, Ben Bagdikian was considered alarmist for pointing this out in his book, *The Media Monopoly*. By 2004, it was down to five conglomerates that controlled most of the country's newspapers, magazines, TV and radio stations, books, records, movies, videos, newswire services and photo agencies.[7] Since then, there have been more mergers and more consolidation of control over the dissemination of information via both traditional sources and new online media. There is simply less and less media democracy.

Another dimension of the problem springs from how journalists have been trained for the last several generations. Journalism schools have worshipped at the altar of "objectivity." Young journalists (myself included, as a 1982 graduate of the University of Wisconsin's School of Journalism) were trained to religiously tell both sides of the story. A worthy pursuit, no doubt. Problem is, sometimes the truth lies on one side. Sometimes the other side does not have a leg to stand on. But in the interest of objectivity, reporters reflexively give equal weight to both sides, filing careful "he said-she said" stories that steer clear of passing judgment on where the truth lies, for fear of appearing biased.

Comedians are under no such restraint. In giving their take on the news, they are at liberty to expose truths that conventional journalists are too often hesitant to reveal. Kids and young adults are not stupid. They have very well-developed bullshit meters. They can discern when the truth is being told and when it is not. Young audiences not only find quality entertainment on The Daily Show and Colbert Report. A great many find more truth there than they find on Fox News, MSNBC or CNN.

There is nothing fair or balanced about outfits like Fox News. But there are still countless journalists who aspire to the journalism school ideal of objectivity. Ironically, their fidelity to this religion has offered them little protection from charges of media bias. In a strange way, it may even invite more such accusations. Working the refs is something coaches in every sport have raised to something of an art form. Get in the ear of the referees or umpires and keep chirping about every call that goes against your team. Give them a good chewing out on the small stuff. Wave your arms, jump up and down, and howl in protest over the big calls that don't go your way. All in hopes of getting them to swallow their whistle later in the game or maybe even give you a make-up call, one that really shouldn't go your way but does.

Works like a charm.

That fact has never gone unnoticed in the political world. Operatives mimic the coaches' behavior, doing their best Bobby Knight impersonations, seeking to bully news reporters and editors into submission. They know the thing journalists value most is their reputation for fairness and objectivity. The Knights of the political world exploit this for all it is worth.

Whenever journalists write or say something that doesn't please the political players, they scream MEDIA BIAS! When enterprising reporters look into apparent wrongdoing, these scoundrels go into hyperdrive to smear the coverage as politically motivated and the newshounds as witch hunters. Most times good reporters show remarkable resistance to these tactics and keep following the scent, despite their understandable anxiety about reputational damage. But sometimes the accusations of bias make them nervous enough to stop barking. And sometimes it's the higher-ups who call off the dogs. In Wisconsin, we saw the state's largest newspaper move a particularly aggressive reporter from the Capitol press corps in Madison to a beat in Milwaukee in what many Capitol watchers saw as an attempt to appease the state's longest-serving governor.

That governor was working the refs. By all outward appearances, it worked. That only inspired more such behavior by the political Knights.

The Knights have the refs badly outnumbered. In Wisconsin's Capitol, hundreds of special interest lobbyists prowl the halls on their clients' behalf. There are just over 130 legislators and hundreds of staffers at their beck and call. Only a handful of journalists work the Capitol beat day in and day out. On a good day, you'll find maybe three or four reporters making use of the Capitol press room.

For as long as anyone can remember, when you walk into the press room you'd see a bank of mailboxes just inside the door to the left. The evolution of those mailboxes over the years has provided a visual depiction of the shrinkage of the Capitol press corps. For years there was a painted wooden structure mounted on the wall with individual boxes for all of the media organizations using the press room. Over the years, as newspapers were consolidated or went out of business altogether, and as fewer radio stations maintained news gathering operations, more and more of the boxes went unused. A political news service editor who was the unofficial but universally accepted dean of the press corps started covering the unused boxes with duct tape. The unsightly appearance of the mailboxes apparently reached a tipping point when half of the boxes were duct-taped shut. The old structure was torn from the wall and replaced by a more elegant mail receptacle with far fewer boxes. Not more than a year or two passed before the bottom two rows were no longer being used.

Newspapers seem to be going the way of the dinosaur. That not only leaves their readers in a tough spot, but also the radio news industry. The running joke has been that radio wouldn't know what to do without newspapers because what passed for a newscast was just the host of the station's news show reading from the morning paper. The television industry as it functions today is way too conflicted by its own financial interests to ever be a dependable source of news about government and politics, especially on the topic of money's stranglehold on public officials. As discussed in chapter 11, the sale of advertising time to politicians and political groups has grown exponentially and has become an addictive revenue stream for TV stations. In the interest of continuing to feed the addiction, they have grown allergic to reporting on the single most corrupting force in American politics.

Young people are not stupid. They notice these things.

There was a time when more or less all Americans shared common sources of news. The entire nation shared the experience of hearing Walter Cronkite describe the day's most notable events before intoning, "And that's the way it is." Cronkite had little choice but to play it straight because of the diversity of his mass audience. Today the news business has become tribalized, with each news outlet appealing to niche audiences. It is now possible to get all of your news from sources that reinforce your biases and cater to your prejudices. That is not to say that our estrangement from "that's the way it is" news is entirely a choice.

The ruling class has turned many a good news operation into an instrument of propaganda. Where they could not bring existing newsrooms and journalists into their service, they set about creating their own. An extensive network of online state news services and virtual Capitol bureaus—from *Colorado Watchdog* and *Pennsylvania Independent* to the *Wisconsin Reporter*—was established by the lofty-sounding Franklin Center for Government and Public Integrity.[8] The Franklin Center was launched by the plutocratic Sam Adams Alliance in 2009 and has ties to an intricate web of right-wing think tanks, conservative sugar daddies, corporate titans, and Republican political operatives and officials.[9]

As traditional media outlets scale back coverage of state politics, the Franklin Center—headed by a former North Dakota Republican Party chief—is happy to step into the breach. The center claims it now provides 10% of all daily news reporting in 38 states.[10] It is hard to say which part of that claim is more debatable—that the center's satellites account for a tenth of all statehouse coverage or that it qualifies as news reporting.

Former *Reuters* chief White House correspondent Gene Gibbons wrote that the Franklin Center's news services are at "the forefront of an effort to blur the distinction between statehouse reporting and political advocacy"[11] and are central to a movement aimed at "delivering political propaganda dressed up as journalism."[12] On a sliding scale of highly ideological, somewhat ideological, and non-ideological, the Pew Research Center's Project for Excellence in Journalism ranked the Franklin Center's online news services "highly ideological."[13]

While the propagandists ambitiously build their capacity, mainstream news organizations cut back on staff and on the news content they deliver. Newspaper pages have shrunk and their "news holes" are smaller as advertising takes up a larger proportion of the available space. On the airwaves—which are public property, by the way—a junk food diet is delivered to the hungry masses. Local newscasts seem more intent on entertaining than educating. What little time is devoted to public affairs is most often spent on pundits telling us what to think instead of reporters giving us important information to think about. And come election time, we are fed a steady diet of political ads full of distortions and smears. The architects of our society's third stage of ownership, their minions in public office and apologists in academia like to say that all these ads are good for us, even going so far as to call them "multivitamins for democracy," as one University of Wisconsin political scientist did. The more advertising the better because it creates a more informed electorate.[14]

Excuse me, but how do scurrilous claims, half-truths, character assassination and outright lies leave us one bit more "informed?" The third stagers' retort is that voters are smart enough to see through lies and figure out who's telling the truth and who's not. But what if no one is telling the truth? Are slander and deception and duplicity and crookedness still politically nutritious?

Lying is not new to politics. What is new is the ever-expanding ability of candidates and their surrogates to do end runs around traditional truth meters and deliver unfiltered lies directly to voters. In the past, politicians delivered their campaign messages through a medium. When they told a whopper, there were trained journalists who researched the statement's validity. If it was found to be untrue or even highly misleading, the claim was often never reported. If it was passed along, it came with the appropriate background information allowing its validity to be judged. No more.

Now if you have enough money you can bypass the truth testers and buy your way straight into voters' living rooms with a pack full of lies. You won't be held accountable. You'll even have allies in what looks an awful lot like newsrooms who bless your deeds and repeat your lies, and some professor somewhere will say what you did was actually good for democracy and a godsend to the voting public.

Unless we want our entire population to become allergic to voting, we had better fight tooth and nail against the consolidation of media ownership in fewer and fewer hands and make an all-out push in the opposite direction—toward media democracy. The broadcast airwaves do not belong to Disney or General Electric or Rupert Murdoch. They are public property. They belong to all of us. It is up to us to reclaim what is rightfully ours.

By so doing, we could restore meaning to the Communications Act of 1934 and enforce that federal law's requirements that broadcasters serve the public interest. Broadcasters could be compelled to meaningfully cover public affairs. Candidates for office could be liberated from the demeaning reality that defines modern politics, namely that to seriously compete for public office in our country nowadays you either must be able to draw upon a personal fortune or be willing to take out a second mortgage on your soul. Either way, you spend a bundle and people conclude you bought the office. One way, we end up with a House of Lords. The other, a House of Whores. This is the *Cash*-22 of contemporary American politics.

While most campaign finance reforms seek to address the *supply* of political money, the kind of reform suggested here takes aim at the *demand* for political money. It would help put the "r" back in free speech, allowing political candidates to communicate with voters without first having to put out the red light. Just like almost every other of the world's democracies already do.

Seeking to take back the airwaves will not sit well with the media monopolies. Expect those who are profiteering on democracy to unleash a lobbying blitzkrieg to keep the gravy train rolling. But if we play our hand right in the digital age—and remember, we hold a valuable trump card in a free and open Internet, if we can keep it— we have it in our power to bust the media trusts.

Additionally, in this age of e-books and blogs and online journals, we all have the means to be publishers. It is no longer necessary to be wealthy enough to buy ink by the barrel. If the truth isn't being reported on the news, we can tell the truth to each other. A printing press isn't required. A PC or laptop or tablet will do.

As with the task of inventing a new political brand and at least one party that is worth a damn, the success of efforts to reinvent news and promote media democracy will come down to the willingness of citizens to come to terms with our feelings of powerlessness and reassert our sovereignty. That starts with recognizing how much sovereignty we've surrendered. It continues with a reawakening to the things we need in order to assert sovereignty. Real news and democracy go hand in hand. One cannot live without the other. That's the way it is.

CHAPTER 13
CHOOSING
WHO CHOOSES

Winning comes easy if you get to make the rules of the game. So it is with our congressional and state legislative elections. Our lawmakers are empowered to design the districts they end up being elected to represent, and not surprisingly they fashion jurisdictions tailor-made for their own re-election. In a democracy, voters are supposed to choose their representatives, not the other way around. In America, it's the other way around.

Redistricting needs to happen. Populations grow and some areas grow faster than others. To make sure each member of the U.S. House of Representatives or any state's legislature represents roughly the same number of people, district boundaries need to be changed periodically to account for population shifts. But just because the task is necessary does not mean that it needs to be done in a way that is harmful to democracy. Gerrymandering—shorthand for politicians abusing the refashioning of legislative districts every 10 years after each census—is not a new phenomenon. The term dates back to 1812, when Massachusetts Governor Elbridge Gerry signed into law a redistricting plan that heavily favored his party. The shape of one of the congressional districts was said to have resembled a salamander.[1]

One gerrymandering technique is called "packing." This is where the party controlling redistricting packs as many of the opposition party's voters into as few districts as possible, intensely concentrating their voting power in isolated areas and widely dispersing it across the rest of the state. Another technique is "cracking." That is when the controlling party breaks apart natural communities of interest—such as minority populations—to dilute their political power and deny them representation.

These age-old practices used to be a dark art. Now, with sophisticated GPS-aided computerized mapping technologies, it is a twisted science. A blunt tool has been honed to razor sharpness. Gerry-style handiwork now is done with never-before-seen precision. And it hits democracy like a ton of bricks.

Representatives choosing their voters inevitably produces lopsided districts—either decidedly Democratic or safely Republican. There are very few evenly divided districts, and consequently precious few truly competitive elections.

Lopsided districts naturally produce legislatures full of fierce partisans and ideological purists. Lost are the moderates who help broker compromise. Left in their absence is polarization. And partisan gridlock. And budget stalemates. You have what we have today in Congress and what we have in my home state—Democrats and Republicans who are unwilling and unable to constructively talk with each other.

Iowa is one place that has found a better way. Iowa's approach takes redistricting out of the hands of self-interested lawmakers and authorizes a nonpartisan legislative service agency to draw new political boundaries, with the proviso that political considerations—including past election results and even the home addresses of current office holders—must be ignored.

The state senator who chairs the committee dealing with any legislation proposing to make changes to the redistricting process in Wisconsin dismisses Iowa's nonpartisan approach to redistricting as "nonsense" and cites one study that speculates that "taking redistricting out of the hands of a unified legislature and giving it to a bipartisan or judicial commission could result in less competitive elections."[2]

What she glosses over is the fact that of Iowa's four U.S. House districts, two rank among the 20 most competitive of the country's 435 congressional districts while none of Wisconsin's eight House districts can be found among the 50 most competitive.[3] In fact, none of Wisconsin's congressional elections in 2012 were competitive. All were won by double-digit margins.[4]

In Wisconsin's 2012 elections Democratic candidates collectively won the most votes for U.S. House, state Senate and state Assembly, but Republicans won the most seats in all three legislative bodies. Not coincidentally, the Republicans controlled the redistricting process after the 2010 census. Across the border in Illinois, the Democrats controlled redistricting and, lo and behold, Democrats maintained control of the statehouse in the Land of Lincoln after the 2012 elections.

The way redistricting is handled currently in Wisconsin and most other states badly weakens voters, thwarts the public's will, and virtually cements in place those already holding office. It's good for the politicians and bad for the voting public. In the most recent redistricting done in Wisconsin in 2011, an added kick to the groin came with the revelation that the public paid dearly for the maneuvers that ensured their electoral wishes were not reflected in the makeup of the legislature. Over $2 million in taxpayer funds were used to pay to draw the maps and then defend them in court.[5]

Nationally, a memo issued by the Republican State Leadership Committee openly boasted that its aggressive gerrymandering campaign known as the Redistricting Majority Project (REDMAP) was responsible for the party maintaining a House majority despite getting fewer votes overall in 2012 congressional elections. Republicans caught Democrats with their pants down, using REDMAP to outspend its Democratic counterpart by a three-to-one margin in the 2010 midterm elections. When the smoke cleared, the GOP had nearly doubled the number of states with total Republican control of legislatures, allowing them to unilaterally redraw district lines in a way that enabled the party to win more House seats across the country despite earning fewer votes than the Democrats.[6]

It is difficult to feel sympathy for the Democrats, however. In Wisconsin, Democrats controlled both houses of the legislature in 2009 and 2010 and were begged by good government advocates and newspaper editorialists to reform redistricting by establishing an independent authority to redraw the political boundaries after the 2010 census. Veteran Democratic lawmakers insisted that the job of redistricting should be done by legislators. Their party's leaders stonewalled the initiative and ultimately succeeded in running out the clock on the legislative session without taking action on redistricting. They clearly were salivating at the prospect of being in a position to unilaterally draw gerrymandered maps to cement their grip on power. Their mouths went dry in a hurry once that fall's election results came in.

While the Republicans clearly got the best of the Democrats in the latest round of redistricting—in Wisconsin and in most states—it is equally clear that both parties know how to gerrymander and both will do it shamelessly if given the chance. Both are occasionally bitten in the backside when their opponents use the weapon against them, yet both are more than willing to play Russian roulette every 10 years. For voters, there is always a bullet in every chamber.

If your idea of democracy involves having citizens in the driver's seat, partisan redistricting done by elected officials is lethal. A simple choice is before us. We either can have voters choosing representatives, or representatives choosing voters. If you are OK with the latter, then states like Wisconsin and Illinois and plenty of others are showing the way. If you prefer the former, then approaches like Iowa's need to be emulated. When commoners band together, establish a new identity and emerge as a force in American politics, one of the causes they will embrace is the establishment of politically independent redistricting authorities all across the country.

CHAPTER 14
BLINDFOLDS AND IMBALANCES

Imagine calling a female coworker a "bitch" and threatening to destroy her, and then calling another coworker a snake ("viper" to be exact), and finally finding yourself in a physical altercation with a third that ended with your hands on her throat. You would most likely, as an attorney specializing in employment law put it, "not last the day."[1]

A Wisconsin Supreme Court justice did all those things and remained on the bench. Several of his colleagues on the court, including two of his ideological allies, suggested he needed counseling.[2] The court system's self-policing agency, the state Judicial Commission, launched an investigation into Justice David Prosser's behavior, but it soon became clear that any misconduct proceedings were a dead end. You see, the state Supreme Court is the final arbiter in judicial misconduct cases in Wisconsin, and the state's judicial ethics code prohibits judges from deciding cases when they witnessed the events under dispute. All but one of the seven justices were in the room when the angry exchange between Prosser and Justice Ann Walsh Bradley culminated with Prosser's hands on Bradley's neck. Most of Prosser's colleagues disqualified themselves

MIKE McCABE

from ruling on the Judicial Commission's findings, citing the code, and the court lacked the needed quorum to judge the case and determine whether discipline was in order.[3]

Before becoming a laughingstock, Wisconsin's Supreme Court had a reputation as one of the nation's finest.

A study published by the UC Davis Law Review showed there was substance behind the perception. Examining more than 60 years worth of decisions by state supreme courts nationwide, the study demonstrated the respect Wisconsin's high court commanded. From 1940 through 2005, its rulings were adopted or relied upon by courts in other states no fewer than 660 times, making it one of the most influential in the nation.[4]

The bloom started coming off the rose in 2007. That's when an open seat on the officially nonpartisan court prompted a highly partisan electoral bloodbath. Nearly $6 million was spent on the election—over four times more than Wisconsin had ever seen spent on a Supreme Court race. The candidates broke all the previous records for fundraising and spending, but were outspent handily by four interest groups that had previously concentrated on influencing elections for partisan offices like governor, legislature and attorney general. Leading the way was the state chamber of commerce, which spent more than $2 million on advertising in the contest.[5]

One look at the candidates' donors stripped away any pretense of nonpartisanship. Whereas high court candidates in Wisconsin had previously relied almost exclusively on donations from colleagues in the legal community, the donor lists in the 2007 race resembled those of candidates for assembly or senate or governor. Organized labor weighed in heavily on one side and business interests countered aggressively on the other. Wisconsin had never seen the likes of it in a judicial election.[6]

The business lobby's favored candidate won, despite being accused weeks before the election of judicial misconduct for repeatedly ruling as a circuit court judge on cases in which she or her husband had a significant financial or business relationship with one of the parties. It didn't take long for the chamber's investment to start paying off. It intervened on behalf of a member company—the paper and packaging giant Menasha Corporation—in a case involving a dispute over whether computer software purchased by a business should be taxed. A lower court said it should. The state Supreme Court reversed that decision, with chamber-backed Justice Annette Ziegler supplying the deciding vote in a 4-3 ruling and writing the opinion overturning the lower court just a year after the business group had spent over $2.2 million to help get her elected. The ruling benefited chamber members to the tune of $300 million.[7]

The Judicial Commission charged Ziegler with violations of the judicial ethics code for her earlier indiscretions as a trial court judge, and eventually her peers on the high court agreed with the commission's findings and made Ziegler the first Supreme Court justice in Wisconsin history to be found guilty of judicial misconduct. Punishment options ranged from censure to suspension to removal from the bench. Despite the historic gravity of the situation, her colleagues settled on a formal reprimand.

Few imagined it possible, but the 2008 election was worse. Wisconsin's first and only African American justice, Louis Butler, stood for election against a business-backed local judge, Michael Gableman. The race was even more expensive, shattering the spending record set just one year earlier. This time, outside interest groups did four-fifths of the campaign spending. The candidates were reduced to little more than bystanders in their own election.[8]

But it was the nature of the advertising that was most horrifying. And it was Gableman's own opening salvo in the ad wars that set the tone for the entire campaign. His smear of Butler was offensive on multiple levels. It played fast and loose with the facts and leaned heavily on deceptive insinuations, implying that Butler had released a convicted child molester who proceeded to rape another child. The ad failed to mention that Butler was not the judge in the case, but rather a public defender. It also neglected to point out that

MIKE McCABE

the convicted criminal was not released from prison early. The second crime was committed only after the full sentence for the first one was served. On top of intentionally misleading viewers, the ad's visual imagery made a not-so-subtle appeal to racism that evoked memories of the infamous Willie Horton ad in the 1988 presidential campaign.[9]

That's not all that was wrong with Gableman's ad. It committed the same act of violence against public understanding of the Supreme Court's role in our justice system as the barrage of interest group ads. Virtually all of the advertising in the 2008 race created the impression that fighting crime is the primary if not sole function of the Supreme Court, as if candidates for the high court were running for sheriff or district attorney. But Supreme Court justices are not sheriffs or DAs. And the Supreme Court is not a trial court responsible for conducting trials and sentencing convicted criminals. It is an appeals court that deals almost exclusively with civil cases, not criminal ones.

Enough Wisconsin voters were persuaded that a crime fighter was needed on the high court and elected Gableman. The Judicial Commission found his Willie Hortonesque ad in violation of the judicial ethics code and filed charges of judicial misconduct against him. Unlike what happened with Ziegler, Gableman's six colleagues on the court deadlocked, refused to embrace the commission's findings, and took no disciplinary action.

So many things about the 2007 and 2008 Supreme Court elections in Wisconsin—the cost, the naked partisanship, the special interest influence, the ugliness—were shocks to the system. Calls to end judicial elections came not only from lawyers and lower court judges but also from newspaper editorialists and other prominent opinion leaders.

Lost in the clamor for an overhaul of judicial selection methods was the fact that Wisconsin had been electing Supreme Court justices for over 150 years. For a century and a half, those elections produced one of the nation's most respected and influential high courts.

Elections were not the problem. That Supreme Court elections were turned into auctions, starting in 2007, was.

Wisconsin is not alone in facing severe threats to the independence of courts and the impartiality of judges. In a series of reports, the national court-reform group Justice at Stake chronicles menaces to judicial integrity—some much worse than those found in Wisconsin—in every part of the country.[10]

Among these stories, a West Virginia episode that inspired John Grisham's novel *The Appeal* stands out. The circumstances bear a striking resemblance to the Menasha Corporation case in Wisconsin but certainly gained greater national notoriety. Massey Coal Company was sued by an industry competitor for unfair and illegal business practices, and a lower court passed down a $50 million judgment against Massey Coal. The company's chief executive Don Blankenship was not going to take this lying down. He spent $3 million getting Judge Brent Benjamin elected to the West Virginia Supreme Court and Benjamin went on to hear Massey's appeal and cast the deciding vote to overturn the $50 million verdict against Blankenship's company. The case wound its way all the way to the U.S. Supreme Court, which ruled in 2009 in *Caperton v. Massey* that Justice Benjamin had a conflict of interest so profound this his participation in the case denied the other side a fair trial and violated the constitutional right to due process.[11]

Caperton prompted states to revisit their judicial ethics codes.[12] A mere four months after the nation's high court rendered its decision, Wisconsin's Supreme Court amended its rules. Instead of taking *Caperton* to heart, the court adopted—verbatim—language proposed by the state chamber of commerce and the statewide association of real estate agents allowing judges to hear and rule on cases involving their biggest campaign supporters. That's right: the court allowed two of the most powerful lobbying groups in Wisconsin to write a major new portion of the state judicial ethics code and blessed it without changing so much as a word.

In 2007 the chamber spent about $2.2 million getting Annette Ziegler elected to the Supreme Court. The following year, the business lobby spent at least another $1.8 million to help put Michael Gableman on the bench. When the next real-life case involving the chamber comes before the court, the new rules the chamber wrote with the realtors will allow Ziegler and Gableman to judge the matter even though one of the parties has $4 million invested in having them on the court.

In *Caperton v. Massey*, the U.S. Supreme Court ruled that spending $3 million to elect a judge in West Virginia and then having that judge hear your case so grossly violated the guarantee of due process and the right to a fair trial that it was unconstitutional. If what happened in West Virginia was unconstitutional, then spending $4 million to elect two judges and having those judges take part in deciding your case must be too. The majority of Supreme Court justices in Wisconsin did not see it that way, however. They chose to just ignore *Caperton*, and so far they've gotten away with it.

Allowing judges to sit on cases involving their biggest campaign supporters is wrong on its face. That the Wisconsin Supreme Court's majority allowed two powerful lobbying groups to write these new ethics rules for them adds insult to injury. And as the U.S. Supreme Court's decision in *Caperton* makes very clear, the conduct being permitted in Wisconsin tramples one of our most basic legal rights. Along the way, it further trashes the reputation of what used to be regarded as one of the nation's most distinguished courts.

Elections have been turned into auctions, and this reality is not only affecting those who make our laws but also those who interpret and enforce them. In 2009 Wisconsin did take a stab at overhauling the financing of Supreme Court elections, but as discussed in chapter 3, the reform was obstructed and ultimately repealed before it could fully take effect.

So for the time being, we are left with judicial candidates who are bystanders in their own elections. No one running for any office is comfortable with bystanding. Bystanders have a way of becoming road-kill in politics. Candidates in judicial elections now have two choices, both of them lousy. They can steer clear of financial conflicts that will compromise them as a judge. But then they surrender control over their electoral destiny and most likely lose. Or they can join the money chase, but then be dogged by conflict-of-interest charges and have their independence as a jurist constantly—and rightly—called into question. They're damned if they do and damned if they don't.

Justice is supposed to be blind. But the current system of choosing who wears the robe strips away the blindfolds. It's become painfully obvious that judges like Brent Benjamin and Annette Ziegler and way too many others can see perfectly well who is buttering their bread.

The judiciary is supposed to be a separate and coequal branch of government that serves as a crucially important check on the power of the executive and legislative branches. Even in a state whose highest court was as esteemed as Wisconsin's, signs are plenty that all branches are under the same spell and consequently there's not much checking going on.

As noted in chapter 4, Wisconsin's Supreme Court blessed a union-busting law that was passed in flagrant violation of the state's open meetings law. As you may recall, Justice David Prosser, the former house speaker, the one in need of counseling, reasoned that the lower court judge erred when he struck down the legislature's actions based on a law that Prosser insisted applies to the legislature unless the legislature says it does not.

After Scott Jensen, Prosser's good friend and successor as speaker, was convicted of felony misconduct in office for his role in the caucus scandal, despite having Prosser as a character witness,[13] he was granted a new trial on a technicality and was allowed to drag out the case for eight years. That was long enough for the legislature to pass a law allowing state officials to face trial in their home counties rather than in the county where crimes were alleged to have occurred, the way it is for every other citizen. The high court then allowed the new law to retroactively apply to Jensen's case despite the fact he had been originally charged and convicted years before the law creating a home court advantage for politicians was enacted. The change of venue to his home turf yielded a plea agreement dismissing felony charges and settling the matter with a civil forfeiture.[14]

In 2010 Prosser's campaign issued a statement saying that if he was reelected to the high court in the spring of 2011, he would serve as "a common sense complement to both the new administration and Legislature."[15] So much for checks and balances. So much for judicial independence.

Courts matter. Judges matter. Most of us don't seem to think so—witness how we're lucky if 20% of voters bother to show up in Wisconsin for state Supreme Court elections—but it matters who sits in judgment of the great disputes of the day. Our way of life and the nature of our society have been shaped to a profound degree by our nation's judges.

Think about the impact four rulings of the United States Supreme Court—arguably the worst four in American history—have had on us and our democracy. Even though these decisions are in most cases generations old, we wrestle to this day with their implications.

In 1857, the nation's highest court ruled in *Dred Scott v. Sanford* that a person can be property, giving the institution of slavery a judicial stamp of approval and constitutional legitimacy. That ruling played a significant role in propelling our nation into civil war only a few years later. Hundreds of thousands died and many more suffered unspeakable trauma in *Dred Scott*'s wake. In too many places and in so many respects, the war is still raging.

In 1886, the accidental precedent established in *Santa Clara County v. Southern Pacific Railroad* led to the acceptance that property can be a person, granting corporations the same rights as individual citizens under the Fourteenth Amendment. *Santa Clara* looms over us today after fathering *Citizens United*.

In 1896, in *Plessy v. Ferguson*, the Supreme Court upheld the constitutionality of racial segregation under the doctrine of "separate but equal." More than half a century later, Martin Luther King and Medgar Evers and so many others who were not yet born when the court so ruled lost their lives while trying to undo that miscarriage of justice.

And then in 1976, the court ruled in *Buckley v. Valeo* that money is speech, transforming the First Amendment's free speech protections from a right that is supposed to belong to all Americans into a privilege that must be purchased at great expense.

All four of those rulings inflicted enormous harm and left the psyche of American democracy deeply scarred. The four courts that rendered these decisions left behind a dishonorable legacy that haunts us still, despite the fact that two of the four rulings—*Dred Scott* and *Plessy*—have fallen by the wayside, swept away by time and experience and enlightenment. The proliferation of hate groups in the wake of the election of our nation's first African American president is proof enough that the mindset that was at the heart of the *Dred Scott* and *Plessy* rulings lives on.[16] And it barely needs mentioning that the doctrines established in *Santa Clara County* and *Buckley* still stand. Corporations are still treated as people under the law, and money is still legally equated with speech.

This history continually collides with the average citizen's hope for a richer, more authentic democracy where people matter more than property. Like it or not, courts and judges will have a great deal to say about when—or even if—we can bring about a day when hope and history marry. So we must act as if courts and judges matter. The success of any new first-party movement will depend in no small part on the restoration of equal access to justice. Reform of recusal rules requiring automatic disqualification of judges with conflicts of interest[17] and an overhaul of the system used for judicial selection needs to be on the to-do list. Where seats on the bench are being auctioned, the selection process needs to be turned back into elections. Where judges are appointed, they need to be selected based on merit, not political connections.[18]

MIKE McCABE

CHAPTER 15

COMMON SCHOOLING

She told me her name was Jennifer. Over the phone her voice sounded young, but what was most striking was its tone—intermittently exuberant and weary. She apologized for bothering me and said she realized I must be terribly busy. (I was not.) She seemed to be bracing herself for rejection, knowing that I had no idea who she was, but screwed up the courage to ask anyway. She wondered if I would be willing to meet with her. She had some questions about politics she wanted to ask.

We arranged a time for her to stop by the Democracy Campaign office. Jennifer had recently graduated from Madison West High School, class of 1999. She had started college, at the University of Wisconsin. She was buoyant and bright-eyed, but in her voice there still was that fatigued, frustrated undertone.

After introducing herself, this full-of-promise Latina fidgeted for a moment, looked down at her hands, then glanced up and blurted, "I don't know anything... you know, about how the government works."

I laughed. I don't know why. Maybe her candor caught me off guard. I mean, how often do you hear someone admit such a thing? And why was she admitting it to me? But laughing was cruel, I know.

My face flushed, my outward display of inwardly kicking myself for the breach of etiquette. Jennifer was undaunted. "No, really, I don't know how it works. They didn't teach us anything in school."

I was impressed by her honesty but even more by her composure, and tried to regain mine. I asked how she came to contact me. The mother of a friend had brought my work to her attention, she said. I asked her to elaborate on her school experience. Much to my astonishment, Jennifer said she had not had a single class dealing with government in her entire time in high school. She sheepishly confessed that her circle of friends all had steered clear of the subject in their course selections, and that she had gone along so she could be in the same classes with them. I first expressed skepticism that a high school diploma could be earned without taking so much as a single civics class, and she assured me it was possible. I then expressed amazement that there evidently wasn't some kind of iron clad requirement, and she emphasized that her experience was the norm, not the exception. None of her peers took any civics classes, she claimed.

We went on to have a lengthy conversation. All these years later, whatever experiences or insights I shared with Jennifer that day are not memorable. While we stayed in touch for a brief time after that first meeting, I cannot say whether our exchanges ever made much of an impression on her. But she made an impression on me. All these years later, I still can hear her say—in that exuberantly frustrated tone of hers—*they didn't teach us anything in school.*

Jennifer's high school is not a failing school. The vast majority of the student body at West High School is college bound. West High produces more National Merit Scholars than any school in Wisconsin, a state whose students perennially earn some of the nation's highest scores on college entrance exams.[1] In many respects, Madison's West High School is exceptional. But in one very important way, it is completely normal. It primarily focuses on serving the needs of our economy, not our democracy.

American schools concern themselves more with producing skilled workers than good citizens because of strong public and political demand to do so. A crucial turning point in American education came in the early 1980s with the publication of *A Nation at Risk*, a report by President Reagan's National Commission on Excellence in Education sounding a warning bell that the United States' education system was failing to produce a competitive workforce. The report resonated because Americans could see looming on the horizon the emergence of an increasingly global economy and stiff international competition that would threaten the country's standing as the world's foremost economic superpower. Filled with anxiety about the nation's ability to keep pace, schools came under intense pressure to place ever greater emphasis on math and science and technology and vocational preparation. "School to work" programs became all the rage. Old classrooms were converted to computer labs.

All of this is perfectly understandable. But it also must be understood that civic instruction fell by the wayside as requirements for more hours of math and science and the addition of technology classes and vocational training took hold. The public and the politicians did not embrace one of the other key recommendations in *A Nation at Risk*—longer school days and a longer school year—so something had to give to make room for the new priorities. Jennifer's experience is a reflection of how that room was made.

In pondering the changes to American education since Reagan's commission told us a "rising tide of mediocrity" threatened our nation, it is useful to reflect on how far our school system has strayed from its roots. What today we call public schools originally were known as common schools. Central to the mission of these schools was making democracy possible.

In 1779 Thomas Jefferson proposed *A Bill for the More General Diffusion of Knowledge*, envisioning a system to provide basic education for the mass of the population. Jefferson called for dividing each county into "little republics" with schools into which "all the free children, male and female" would be admitted free of charge.

Civic literacy was at the heart of Jefferson's plan. He emphasized the study of history as a means of cultivating moral and civic virtues and enabling the masses to know and exercise their rights and duties. Articulating a vision that would animate the next century's common school movement, Jefferson conceived of elementary schooling as basic education for citizenship, a public investment in the capacity for self-government. He famously observed, "If a nation expects to be ignorant and free in a state of civilization, it expects what never was and never will be."[2]

Jefferson was hardly alone in his concern about the need for popular education. Many of Jefferson's allies and adversaries alike shared his zeal for the establishment of common schools. After signing his name to the Declaration of Independence, Pennsylvanian Benjamin Rush insisted the revolutionary war was only the "first act of the great drama" and called for a system of schools in his native state. Noah Webster, whose spelling book and dictionary of the English language immeasurably aided the fragile new republic by helping to expand the lettered population, heartily agreed with Rush and Jefferson. A schoolmaster who went on to found Amherst College, Webster considered education to be the most important business of civil society. Webster's dictionary surely can be found in today's school libraries, but his dedication to the school's role in promoting civil society is now missing.[3]

The common school movement really took flight in the 1830s as reformers, often from the Whig Party, called on government to en-sure the schooling of all children. No one played a bigger role in the development of common schools than Horace Mann, the Massachu-setts lawyer and legislator who became secretary of the newly estab-lished state board of education in 1837. With evangelical zeal, Mann pitched free, universal education to the laboring classes as "the great equalizer of the conditions of men, the balance wheel of the social machinery." To the propertied, he preached that their prosper-ity—and security—depended on having literate and law-respecting neighbors. To every audience, Mann declared that the idea of education as the "absolute right of every human being that comes into the world" came not from the minds of men but from Providence.[4]

The idea of schools as first and foremost laboratories of democracy and builders of social capital continued to hold sway as the next century dawned. As discussed in chapter 2, Wisconsin legislators in 1911 blazed trails on an amazing number of policy fronts. Among their ambitions that came to fruition was a law that identified schools as "social centers" where not just students but anyone in the community could gather to discuss the issues of the day and develop solutions to the challenges facing society.[5]

By the mid-1980s, some educators in Wisconsin and presumably elsewhere were openly fretting about the decline of civic education. They persuaded state lawmakers to mandate instruction in state and local government. The mandate was a much-needed gesture, but social studies teachers at the time were ill-equipped to carry it out. National textbook publishers offered next to nothing focusing specifically on government at the local and state levels. Teachers had not received training focused on the subject.

At that time I was directing a civic education program for the nonprofit Wisconsin Taxpayers Alliance. We did our part to fill the instructional materials void by publishing a textbook on Wisconsin government that was widely used in elementary and secondary schools in the state. I served on a state social studies curriculum committee and co-authored a curriculum guide on state and local government for the Wisconsin Department of Public Instruction. I regularly made presentations at teacher-training seminars and gave nearly 700 classroom talks to students on the democratic process and state and local government finance.

Looking back, we were swimming upstream. And the current produced by *A Nation at Risk* was powerful. Ensuring workforce preparedness trumped empowering citizenship. But even putting aside the social and political pressures to emphasize math, science, technology and vocational training, our efforts on behalf of Jefferson's vision were badly flawed. We overemphasized the structure and inner workings of government and its institutions and offices, and comparatively glossed over where citizens fit into the equation. I added a chapter to our textbook entitled "Influencing Your Government," but it was little more than an acknowledgement of an important omission.

To this day, to the extent that we teach democracy at all, it is taught as a spectator sport for most and as job training for a few aspiring public servants. Even at the college level, you can look at the political science course offerings of just about any higher education institution and you will almost certainly find courses focusing on the American presidency, and on Congress, and the court system. There are courses in public administration examining how the bureaucracy works. There are courses on international relations and foreign policy, and courses on a wide range of domestic policy areas, and ones on the finer points of election administration.

It is far less likely that you will find Organizing 101, or an advanced Theory and Practice of Social Movements course, or a Petitioning Your Government practicum. How strange that in a country that boasts of being the world's greatest democracy, we really don't teach democracy. We teach government, reluctantly and tepidly, and we teach it in a way that puts elected officials, appointed bureaucrats, career civil servants, judges and diplomats in the spotlight. We pay occasional lip service to the idea that the highest office in a democracy is that of citizen, but we don't teach democracy that way. The art of being an active and constructive citizen is researched less and taught less by political scientists than any other dimension of their discipline.

The intense push for school privatization discussed in chapter 2 is a major threat to common schooling. At worst, school voucher programs and similar privatization schemes are back-door resegregation ploys. At best, they certainly represent an abandonment of the Providence that Horace Mann spoke of. This abandonment also is reflected in soaring college tuition that leaves most new graduates sentenced to debt and a great many others priced out of the higher education marketplace altogether.

A nation that claims to be a democracy but no longer considers adequate education a universal right and neglects to make citizenship education a priority is one that remains very much at risk.

CHAPTER 16
MILLENNIALS TO THE RESCUE

Back in 2001, I was asked to give the commencement address at the high school graduation ceremony in Evansville, Wisconsin. That is the small town where I spent the early part of my childhood. Evidently a teacher there was familiar with my work for the Wisconsin Democracy Campaign and had heard me speak a time or two. She also was aware I had attended Evansville schools for a number of years, and consequently felt I had the makings of a good commencement speaker.

I often wonder if she still felt that way by the end of that early June evening. Nobody really listens to commencement speeches, and mine was well on its way to being typically unremarkable. Then I reminded the graduates that our country is the creation of revolutionaries. I told them that sometimes we seem to forget this great nation was founded by malcontents. People who got sick and tired of being told what to do. I went on to say that sometimes we forget that Thomas Jefferson said each generation should start a revolution and that he believed every generation should tear up the Constitution and start over. I again quoted Jefferson saying that expecting each new generation to forever live by the customs and laws of past generations is like expecting adults to wear the same clothes that fit them as children.

I concluded my remarks by saying the greatest thing about America is we are never satisfied with the way things are. When we are at our best, I told them, we are still a nation of malcontents and rabble-rousers.

You'd have thought I quoted Hitler, not Jefferson. A few in the audience clapped briefly when I stepped away from the microphone. Most sat silently with furrowed brows. Some parents in the crowd shot me dirty looks. The graduates squirmed in their seats, seemingly not knowing how to respond. School administrators who flanked me onstage looked like they had seen a ghost.

I made one friend that night. A member of the school board, Jeff Conn, caught up to me as I was crossing the parking lot on my way to my car. He told me he loved my speech, but that it had caused quite a stir. His colleagues on the school board were incensed. The school principal and district superintendent were up in arms. I shouldn't expect to ever be invited back, he told me.

Jeff could see I was perplexed by the reaction to the speech. "You have to understand, Mike, they've been telling these kids for four years to sit down, shut up and do as they are told."

Jeff became a loyal supporter of the Democracy Campaign and the two of us kept in touch in the years that followed. But he turned out to be right: I never was invited back to Evansville High School.

By the look of things, the class of 2001 and others who started life or came of age at the dawning of the new millennium will not likely sit down or shut up much longer.

The Millennial generation—today's teens and twenty-somethings—has grown up in an age full of right-wing populists fanning phantom flames of reverse discrimination to incite white, heterosexual, religious, native-born Americans to political action. But they have not bought what these merchants have been selling. One likely reason is that there are comparatively fewer white, Christian non-immigrants in the Millennials' ranks. Forty percent of Millennials are ethnic or racial minorities[1] and under half of them regard religion as "very important" in their lives.[2]

Compared to older Americans, even Millennials who are white, straight, native-born and Christian are less resentful of people who are not any of those things. They are much more likely than older Americans to be accepting of gay rights and marriage equality, and are considerably more comfortable with someone in their family marrying someone of a different race. In fact, they are more liberal on every major social issue except abortion, where there is no notable generation gap.[3]

Millennials are much more likely to be doves on foreign policy. They aren't nearly as willing as older generations to sacrifice civil liberties to fight terrorism and are much less likely to say military force is the best way to combat terrorism.[4]

They are more supportive of labor unions than the population as a whole, and prefer a bigger government offering more services to a cheaper one providing less. Millennials also are much more likely than older Americans to say that business has more control over their lives than government.[5] Perhaps not surprising given their age, Millennials send mixed signals about Social Security, favoring its privatization while also being more likely than past generations of young people to support spending more money on the program.[6]

The under-thirty generation is the only segment of the adult population more likely to describe themselves as "have nots" rather than "haves" and, as briefly noted in chapter 5, Millennials narrowly favor socialism over capitalism while older Americans prefer capitalism by a wide margin. There's good reason for this. The system has never worked for them.

In 2001, as the first Millennials were entering the workforce, the U.S. economy slid into recession. By 2007 the unemployment rate still was above pre-recession levels.[7] Then all hell broke loose. The nation's housing bubble burst, some banks teetered and many others failed, and a massive financial meltdown ensued. By 2012, it was apparent just how bad the timing of the Millennials' entry into the job market had been. From 1989 to 2000, both recent high school and college graduates saw double-digit percentage increases in wages. From 2000 to 2012, wages dropped by 13% for new high school graduates and went down 8% for recent college grads.[8]

To make matters worse, the government offered little shelter from the storm. The country's social safety net was not designed to help young adults. It is harder for younger Americans to qualify for unemployment insurance, food stamps, tax relief from the Earned Income Tax Credit, or grants under the Temporary Assistance for Needy Families program.[9]

In the midst of the bad economy, Millennials also were hit hard by sharp declines in public investments in higher education. In 2012, *The New York Times* reported that state and local spending per college student hit a 25-year low.[10] With less government funding at their disposal, colleges passed along their ever-escalating costs to students and their families in the form of higher tuition and other fees. Millennials borrowed heavily to pay the higher bills. Between 1989 and 2010, the average amount of college debt per household tripled.[11]

America's teens and twenty-somethings have a legitimate ax to grind with the nation's economic and political systems. Against this backdrop, people with a little gray on the roof still often find themselves grumbling about how apathetic young people are. Attend an AARP chapter meeting or a Rotary Club luncheon and chances are you will hear this common refrain. I think they mistake powerlessness for apathy.

In my line of work, I regularly get invited to visit college campuses and high school classrooms. I do not find much apathy there. I do find endemic powerlessness. The two can be easily confused, but are in truth quite different. Apathy is when you do not care. Those who feel powerless may care a great deal about the enormous challenges facing our country, but they do not believe there is a damn thing they can do about any of it.

Many others have taken notice of this condition as well; in fact, its detection has even made it into pop culture. John Mayer put it to song:

> *Me and all my friends, we're all misunderstood;*
>
> *They say we stand for nothing, and there's no way we ever could;*
>
> *Now we see everything that's going wrong, with the world and those who lead it;*
>
> *We just feel like we don't have the means, to rise above and beat it.*

There will come a time when the Millennials will stop waiting on the world to change and start exerting their will to change it. When that happens, they will put their stamp on our politics and economy. Given their attitudes on these matters, America is in for the kind of political remodeling Thomas Jefferson recommended.

CHAPTER 17
HIDDEN TREASURE

If there were bankruptcy protection for politicians, and if they felt even the slightest pangs of either honesty or shame, today's America would be in the midst of an epidemic of Chapter 11 filings. Republicans, with their twisted knack for exalting Jesus in word and Ayn Rand in deed, are on the verge of moral bankruptcy if they have not already arrived. Democrats, having gone decades with nary an original thought, might as well file for intellectual bankruptcy.

We are in a fine mess, democracy-wise. The biggest such mess in living memory. We need to find our way out.

Maps can be found in the unlikeliest places. Today, Wisconsin Dells has the look of the consummate tourist trap. Its boosters proclaim the Dells the waterpark capital of the world. Its streets are lined with amusements parks, a signature attraction featuring the unlikely combination of a water ski show and "science exploratory," an upside-down replica of the White House, miniature golf courses, freak shows and haunted houses, as well as all of the accommodating hotels, restaurants, drinking establishments and souvenir shops.

Underneath this carnival barker exterior is buried treasure—history replete with conquest and corruption and reform and democracy's reclamation, a chapter of which takes us through the place now known as Wisconsin Dells. French explorers who passed through in the 1700s were spellbound by the region's layered stone cliffs and the striped canyons cut by the Wisconsin River and dubbed it the "Dalles"[1]—their word for the rapids of a river running between the walls of a gorge.[2]

The settlement became known as Kilbourn, named for the Milwaukee railroad baron Byron Kilbourn. In its early days, Milwaukee was divided into three burgs, including one known as Kilbourntown.[3] Kilbourn's ambitions were not confined to Milwaukee, however. In the mid-1850s, Kilbourn aspired to build a railroad crossing Wisconsin from Milwaukee to the Mississippi River at La Crosse. He needed land along a corridor spanning the entire width of the state, but did not care to compensate the land owners for their property. Instead, he wanted territorial legislators to use their new powers of eminent domain to condemn the land he needed and give it to him in a land grant.

In return for the legislation, in 1856 Kilbourn offered 13 senators $175,000 in bribes and 59 members of the assembly $355,000 more. According to the historical record, only one senator—a Republican, "Honest" Amasa Cobb—refused the payment. Kilbourn paid Governor Coles Bashford $50,000 to sign the legislation.[4] These were astonishing sums of money at the time, as unskilled laborers were earning well under a dollar a day and the daily wage of trained craftsmen was less than $2. Kilbourn got his free land and built his railroad, crossing the Wisconsin River at what is now Wisconsin Dells. They named the town after him in 1857.

That era's corruption made Wisconsin a national laughingstock. Harper's magazine ran a cartoon showing a railroad president at a "political market," inspecting figurines labeled "Wisconsin Legislature" tied up in bunches for sale and telling the peddler: "I want a

Governor very much indeed. Get me a Wisconsin one, if possible."[5] Such crooked dealings also prompted a citizen revolt.

A crusading newspaperman named Stephen Decatur Carpenter worked for years to expose and condemn the open bribery of lawmakers by railroad tycoons and their lobbyists seeking favors. Nicknamed "Pump" after inventing a device used to drain water from lead mines, Carpenter aimed his choicest words at William Barstow, who was secretary of state and later governor. Carpenter dubbed him and his minions "Barstow and the 40 Thieves" and relentlessly editorialized against their backroom maneuvers to secure favorable railroad legislation.

The public's strong reaction to Carpenter's revelations succeeded in bringing down Barstow. But Bashford soon followed him to power, and Pump Carpenter kept right on crusading. He was vindicated in 1857 when Alexander Randall (for whom the University of Wisconsin Badgers football team's Camp Randall stadium is named) defeated the corrupt Bashford by 118 votes. Carpenter could not contain his satisfaction, splashing these headlines across the front page of his *Wisconsin Patriot* newspaper:

TEN MILLION CHEERS! CROW, OLD ROOSTER! CROW!! THE FORTY THIEVES CLEARED OUT! RANDALL ELECTED GOVERNOR! HONESTY TRIUMPHANT! THERE IS A GOD IN ISRAEL![6]

By the time Carpenter died several decades later, Wisconsin had enacted some of the nation's strongest anti-corruption laws, giving birth to my state's reputation for squeaky clean politics. For more than a century that followed, Wisconsin was known from coast to coast as a beacon of clean, open and honest government. The people living at that Wisconsin River crossing disassociated themselves from the Kilbourn name, opting instead for an Americanized version of the moniker the French explorers had bestowed upon it.

Wisconsin Dells moved on. So did my state. We largely buried the history. Not even in school are the doings of Byron Kilbourn and

Coles Bashford and Honest Amasa Cobb and Pump Carpenter recounted. But they live among us again, assuming new identities.

Wisconsin has come full circle. We now face threats to democracy not seen since the robber barons reigned supreme at the Capitol in the nineteenth century's Gilded Age. Wisconsin once pioneered advances like election-day registration to promote high voter turnout. Now barriers to voting are being steadily erected. Political boundaries are drawn in a way that allows one party to win the most seats in Congress and in the legislature even though the other party gets the most votes.

In 2010 the Supreme Court effectively wiped out Wisconsin's century-old law banning corporate electioneering with its *Citizens United* decision and legalized unlimited election spending throughout the land. Wisconsin saw election spending triple in the aftermath.[7] The system of public financing of state elections that served as a model for the nation for 34 years was repealed. The Impartial Justice Act cleaning up state Supreme Court races was dumped after just one election.

If money is speech, as the Supreme Court insists it is, then never before have so few spoken at such a deafening volume. Donations as large as half a million dollars from a single individual to a Wisconsin governor look conspicuously like the bribes Pump Carpenter spilled so much ink over.[8]

Here in Wisconsin, what we are left with is the best governing money can buy. Mining interests say dig, and officials marinated in pro-mining money dutifully say "how deep?" and get cracking on legislation to loosen mining regulations. Corporations dangle expansion plans in front of state officials and are showered with tax breaks and offers of subsidized loans, grants and other welfare for the rich. Road builders bellyache about others making claims on the taxpayer funds they want in order to pour ever more concrete, then proceed to throw around some serious cash, and lawmakers snap to attention and promptly work on rewriting the state constitution to create

MIKE McCABE

special protection for the road budget that no other state program or service enjoys.

Year after year, wealthy school privatization backers shower campaign support on Wisconsin officials, and darned if public school budgets don't get shaved and more and more public money gets steered to expanded private school voucher programs.

The subjects of Carpenter's ire—namely Barstow and Bashford and the 40 Thieves—are long gone. But the behavior he railed against has come back to haunt Wisconsin and your homeland in this day and age. Pump Carpenter would know us well.

As disheartening as current conditions are, we can take comfort and draw inspiration from our history. It's an antidote to the cynicism that has grown like a cancer in so many of our souls. We face nothing today that hasn't been faced—and defeated—before. Right on this soil. Defeated by people who had so much less going for them then than we do now. They had far less wealth. Few were property owners. The most skilled among them were earning $2 a day. They had less education. Few had high school diplomas and many were illiterate. They had fewer means of communication. There was no TV. No radio. No Internet, obviously. The printing press was their only instrument of mass communication. They were up against vast wealth and power concentrated in a very few privileged hands. And they beat the greedy bastards. In so doing, they set Wisconsin on a path that made it synonymous with clean government and progressive politics that lasted better than a century. This was my inheritance. It was handed down to all who call this place home. We have pissed away the bequest.

So we again stand at a crossroads. But we stand here with the knowledge that conditions like today's have been faced before... and overcome. If they could do it then, we can do it now. We don't have to make history. We only have to repeat it.

CHAPTER 18
THE SECRETS TO OUR SALVATION

It all comes down to two forgotten currencies.

The political establishment is operating as if there is only one currency in American politics—namely money. They are fixated on that currency. Most who are not professional political operatives have been brainwashed into thinking that money is the only currency. That brainwashing leaves people who don't have a lot of cash to throw around in the political arena feeling powerless. Political powerlessness has the same effect as clinical depression. It is paralyzing. And paralyzed is just what today's political establishment wants the citizenry to be.

There is not just one political currency. There are at least three. Money has great power. But so do organized people and provocative ideas, when properly employed. These currencies need to be put back in circulation.

A paralyzed citizenry is not an organized and engaged citizenry. And citizens will not be inspired to organize and engage when one party is bent on returning us to the nineteenth century and the other's clock seems to have stopped in the twentieth. Provocative twenty-first century thinking will not come from one party that is scary and another that is scared.

America is going through a decades-long process of economic dislocation at least as massive as the Industrial Revolution. We just haven't fully decided what to call it yet. We are fighting seemingly perpetual wars abroad. We are mired in political corruption and dysfunctional governing at home. People are afraid our children's generation will be the first in our nation's history not to be better off than their parents.

When people are afraid, most will gladly trade freedom for security. Look no further than the Patriot Act or the excesses of the NSA for evidence of that. Most will take the comfort of a well-known past over the risk of a yet-to-be-discovered future. Unless, that is, someone both brave and optimistic offers a compelling vision of what lays beyond the horizon. Is there anyone who believes today's Democratic Party is a brave and optimistic party?

The answer to that question is what empowers the "rewinders." I call the gang who've captured today's Republican Party rewinders because they only know how to push the rewind button. Their answer to every problem is to turn back the clock. Their efforts have met with considerable success. As illustrated on these pages, we are reliving the nineteenth century's Gilded Age in so many respects.

But just as we can take comfort and inspiration from history as we face the ongoing struggle between honor and corruption, we also can draw comfort and inspiration from those who came before us and proved themselves unafraid to sail over the horizon. We know what those who sailed before us discovered. There is nothing to fear over the horizon. The earth is round. The rewinders still seem convinced the earth is flat. But it is round.

We have it in our power to create a new political identity and an innovative vision of a bright future on a small scale in places like

Wisconsin and on a grand scale throughout America. Our best days do not have to be behind us. We have it in our power to breathe life back into democracy and put blue jeans in high places.

A moment is upon us when a movement must be built. The people are ready. That both parties are failing America is self-evident. The people are able, even if most don't know it. We have more going for us today than movement builders of yesterday did. The question is whether the people are willing. Movement building is long, hard, uncertain work. The political establishment will not give us a party that is worth a damn. We have to make one. We have to pull ourselves up by our own bootstraps and create what we desire. Nobody is going to do it for us.

In deciding how to move ahead, it is always useful to look back. History is prologue. That being the case, there is no better time than this Stilted Age to ask ourselves: *What would Bob do?*

Fighting Bob La Follette would fight, of course.

He would barnstorm the state. He'd reach out to people just like those who raised me. Working people. Plain folks. People like Les Sturz. But more important than anything, he would eschew tarnished labels and renounce membership in corrupt institutions. He would call himself something new.

La Follette surely would do one more thing. He would call on us to join a great struggle. He would ask us to sacrifice today in order to make possible a better tomorrow.

After 9/11 President Bush told us to go shopping. Talk about your metaphors. Talk about your sharp contrasts. On the heels of the Great Depression, my parents' generation rallied to defeat Nazism. Gas and rubber and sugar and butter and cloth were all rationed. There were scrap metal drives and victory bonds. The whole country was called upon to sacrifice.

What has our whole country been asked to sacrifice? We were exhorted to shop. You know and I know that war and the ones that followed wouldn't have lasted nearly as long—or maybe not been started at all—if we weren't paying for them on a credit card and instead taxes were being raised. Or if there was a draft and all of our families faced the possibility of having a draft-age child sent away to die.

Instead of rallying the whole country as my parents' generation was rallied, our president cynically manipulated us. How we respond to such crass ploys is the great challenge of this moment in time. Our biggest fight is the fight against the greatest enemy of peace, justice and democracy—cynicism.

We need only remember. There is no greater threat to the ruling class, for remembering enables us to imagine. There is no better antidote to the cynicism that has grown like a cancer in so many of our souls. We face nothing today that hasn't been faced—and defeated—before.

OK, you and I can't buy politicians. We can't even afford a good down payment on one. We can't peddle influence. We have no $250-an-hour lobbyists working the halls of the Capitol on our behalf. We can't buy public opinion. We have no PR firms to do polling and craft state-of-the-art marketing campaigns. No 30-second paid advertisements to spread our message. We can't make the news whatever we want it to be. We don't own TV or radio networks.

But there is much we do have. We have the purchasing power of two other currencies. There is much we can do. Regaining our senses is a good place to start. It's said that insanity is doing the same thing over and over and expecting a different result. By that definition, American voters are insane.

Roughly 1% of the population pays for the campaigns of those seeking office. Some Republicans are elected, some Democrats. They proceed to cater to the 1% who paid to put them in office, driving the other 99% up a wall.

Without demanding changes in the way elections are paid for, voters re-elect most of those who drove them crazy. They throw out a few in the interest of shaking things up, in hopes of a different result.

One time it's the Democrats we invest our hopes in, another time it's the Republicans. The newly elected officials got the money for their campaigns from 1% of the people. They continue catering to that fraction of the population. The rest feel let down and left out again.

Another election comes. No changes in the way campaigns are waged and financed have been demanded or made. The same 1% pay for all the ads, all the mailings, all the robocalls. Once again, most of those who were in power stay in power. A few get tossed, maybe a few more than usual. Voters hope against hope for a different result, for some bipartisan cooperation and constructive problem solving, for some consideration of the greater good. Hopes are dashed again. Another election comes. And another. The same thing is done over and over again, yet a different result is somehow expected each time. Insane is what it is.

If American democracy is ever to become, you know, like an actual democracy, we can't keep doing the same thing over and over again, election after election. You and I have to come to terms with the sheer insanity of our past behavior.

There's a sequence to restoring sanity that needs following. **Step one is consciously striving to change our political vocabulary.** This involves fully grasping the bondage of the current vernacular. Consider how often we all refer to politicians as "leaders." In reality, few in society are less involved with leadership than politicians. With a few impressive exceptions, politicians are consummate followers. They don't move a muscle without getting marching orders from their key supporters. They constantly are checking the political currents, poring over polls or convening focus groups to see which way the winds are blowing. Politicians are quick to notice which way the parade is headed and even quicker to run to the front and grab a flag or a drum. Such behavior is a lot of things, but it is not leadership.

There is a public affairs school at the University of Wisconsin named for Fighting Bob La Follette, who famously said that "the will of the people is the law of the land." Not long ago, that school started offering its students a course called "Exercising Political Leadership." According to the course syllabus, the class was to focus on government executives like presidents, governors and mayors and how they "accumulate and spend political capital." That confuses exercising political power with leadership. Common mistake, and one that is particularly in keeping with the times.

Leadership has to be the most overused and abused word in politics. No class of people boasts about leadership more than politicians do. And perhaps no class of people does less actual leading.

While fully acknowledging that it took considerable courage to do it, Lyndon Johnson wasn't leading when he signed civil rights legislation. He was following. The Civil Rights Movement made him do it. Masses of people marched, and endured beatings, and had high-powered fire hoses turned on them, and were jailed, and in some cases gave their lives for the cause. They weren't accumulating or spending political capital—at least not consciously. They were leading. And they changed America.

Just a few short years ago, Wisconsin had an assembly speaker who stood for amending the state constitution to forever ban gay marriage, and whose voice dripped with hate as he mocked "a lot of people out there who think that people should be able to marry whoever they want, or whatever they want." More than a few of his contemporaries cracked wise about how the Bible speaks of "Adam and Eve, not Adam and Steve."

Today politicians of that same stripe are scurrying for cover, dissembling here and waffling there, frantically trying to figure out a way to reposition themselves on gay rights and same-sex marriage. Are they leading? Of course not. They are reading polls. Attitudes are changing. The American people are leading.

In a true democracy, citizens are the cue-givers and the direction-setters. We are the leaders we have been waiting for. So the next time you catch yourself calling one politician or another a "leader," make a conscious effort to choose another word.

The next time you catch yourself talking about liberals and conservatives, and left wings and right wings, make a conscious effort to stop thinking horizontally and start thinking vertically. When we exert control over the way things are talked about, we start to control the way things get done.

Step two is activating the magnet. People don't join anything bigger than a book club or fantasy sports league without a damn good reason. They won't join unless they are convinced there is a problem that demands their attention. Once they reach the conclusion there is system failure that poses a sufficient threat to their life, liberty, property or happiness, they still won't join if they cannot envision a happy ending.

Most Americans are not fans of either major party. We see how they are failing us. Increasingly, we are politically homeless. We are despairing over the condition of our democracy and we'd like to go in and fix it. But too many of us see only two doors, and we have opened them before and we know what is on the other side. Behind door number one is a third party. We've had our dalliances. We got our hopes up on more than one occasion, only to have them dashed each time. Behind door number two are the two major parties. We hold our noses and choose whichever we consider the lesser of two evils.

Movement builders need to make a compelling case that there is another door, one that hasn't been opened in our lifetimes but one that was used by our own ancestors to escape conditions comparable to those revisiting us today. Behind door number three is a new political household where we can take up residence and from where a modern day renovation of one or both of the major parties can be executed. We haven't tried it in our day and age—we haven't even thought about it—but the first-party strategy proved successful on more than one occasion before we came along and got ourselves into our current mess. This knowledge, properly spread, can be the magnet that draws people to the task of shoring up our foundering democracy.

MIKE McCABE

Step three is naming the movement and establishing a new political identity that transcends old caricatures and stereotypes while reflecting and reinforcing the new vocabulary. The Democrats, for example, are seen as the party of big government, the party of handouts, the party that coddles the moochers among us, the party that promises something for nothing. Their enemies' narrative is that there are makers and takers in our society, and the Democrats cater to the takers. On top of that, they portray Democrats as Birkenstock-wearing, Volvo-driving elites. They've turned words like "liberal" and "progressive" into something akin to ethnic slurs.

The instinctive response by establishment Democrats is to become Republican-lite, mimicking the GOP on economics and budgets while drawing some distinctions on social issues. They call pretending to be Republicans with a softer edge "The Third Way." They assume Americans actually want the mongrel offspring of the cross-breeding of elephants and donkeys. They will not come to the Fourth Way on their own. That will require a movement of citizens both demanding and representing something that is neither elephant nor ass.

As noted in chapter 9, the identity of that something needs to be familiar and instantly recognizable. It has to have universal appeal, something that unites us, something that people from every walk of life and every part of America can relate to and identify with. And it needs to symbolize the distinction between the populist movement builders and the ruling class. I throw blue jeans out there as an illustration, but the movement doesn't have to be denim-clad to be successful. Possibilities abound.

Boots. Farmers wear 'em. Construction workers wear 'em. Soldiers wear 'em. They are salt of the earth. When we start thinking vertically and we lose today's garbled code, we stop talking about left and right and liberals and conservatives and we talk instead about royals and commoners or stilts and boots.

Better yet, bootstraps. Everybody, and I mean *everybody*, knows the saying. Pull yourself up by your bootstraps. For first-party insurgents who want to make at least one party that's worth having, what better way to shake the Democratic Party to its foundation than seizing the enemy's narrative, turning it to advantage, and forging an insurgent identity that stands in direct contrast to the negative stereotype.

Step four is to take inventory of both the movement's assets and those of your opponents, and devise a game plan that plays to your strengths and capitalizes on your opponents' weaknesses. The major parties have money and lots of it. As noted, the major parties cannot at the present time recognize any political currency but money. A movement to remake American politics could try to fight fire with fire, but such a strategy almost surely will result in democracy going up in flames. Savvy movement builders will recognize and embrace the fact that there is more than one way to fight fire, and they will focus on equipping themselves with the political equivalent of axes, shovels, ladders, hydrants and hoses.

I repeat: There is not just one currency in American politics. There are at least three. Today's political establishment is so fixated on the money game that it overlooks the power of organized people and the power of big ideas. There always has been highly organized money in politics. Only rarely do people get organized. Those rare occasions have coincided with times just like the ones we are experiencing now. Provocative, powerful ideas are rarer still, especially in times of austerity. Our country has been mired in austerity—both economic and intellectual—for too long now. It's time to think big again. It's time to dream. America can't become what it has the potential to be without big ideas. To give just one example among many, the American Dream is lost unless we dare to liberate our youth from the captivity of student debt and find a way to extend the promise of free public education all the way through college.

The game plan must take into account that many of us have fallen victim to paralyzed thinking, having drawn the conclusion that organizing people and spreading ideas depends on having large sums of money. Money almost certainly trumps either of the other two currencies alone, but history teaches that combining organizing and

MIKE McCABE

creative thinking produces a potent concoction. Just over a century ago, the money power of the Rockefellers and Carnegies and their contemporaries proved no match for aroused masses armed with a new vision of what America should be. The Kochs and Waltons and their ilk will prove no match in our time.

Step five is to think and act locally, with global designs. Establish a universal identity and design a new political household that anyone anywhere can move into. But once that big picture has been drawn, the trick is to think small. Start at the neighborhood level. Then community-wide. Next, knit those emerging networks together with county chapters. Only when those are well established will state chapters emerge. The sum total of what's built in state after state will be a national movement.

Blueprints are important, but they don't build anything. At some point, hammer must be put to nail. We must act, but keep it simple as we do. We will do well to remember and follow the advice of César Chávez, the legendary champion of farm workers and migrant laborers. When a young student asked him for his secret to organizing, Chávez is said to have replied: "The only way I know how to organize is to talk to one person, then talk to another person, then talk to another person."

This is simple advice, but no easy task. We are all taught from an early age that there are two things to avoid talking about in polite company—religion and politics. To meaningfully participate in democracy, you will often encounter the former and absolutely must be willing to discuss the latter.

There is much to talk about. Take your pick. If you want the will of the people to be the law of the land, you can talk to one person and then another about the need for a Twenty-Eighth Amendment to the U.S. Constitution putting the "r" back in free speech and reestablishing that money is not speech, corporations are not people, elections are not auctions, and public offices are not commodities to be bought and sold. You can talk to one person, then another, about how Net Neutrality must be protected at all costs so we can continue to have a free and open Internet and so some future hand-held device can revolutionize our democracy once television is no longer the dominant means of political communication.

You can talk to one person, and another and another, about the need to break up the media monopolies, or the need to take redistricting out of the hands of the politicians and give it to an independent authority so voters can choose their representatives and not the other way around. You can talk about how much more responsive to us our representatives would be if we had publicly financed campaigns creating voter-owned elections instead of the donor-owned ones we have now.

But regardless of how the conversation is started, it needs to lead to a discussion about how to create at least one party that is worth a damn, at least one that could be counted on to do the people's will on any of the things that matter to that one person with whom you are speaking. At least one party not represented by a nineteenth century symbol. A new political brand suited to our times, a new political identity befitting us.

Step six is to challenge establishment politicians in their own party primaries. Use the new brand and big ideas and the organization built neighborhood by neighborhood, community by community, and county by county to offer voters who have been holding their noses at the polls a breath of fresh air. Here again, think local. Establish the new brand at the community level by getting movement-endorsed candidates elected to local offices. This is the farm system where candidates for higher offices will be found and developed.

These six steps have the potential to hit the political landscape with the force of an earthquake, much like the quakes that shook the ground the parties stood on twice previously in America. But history does not make itself. It must be made, of course.

Very recently, I was invited to speak on the University of Wisconsin's satellite campus in Oshkosh along the shores of Lake Winnebago. After finishing my remarks about the growing threats to democracy and the compromised health of our political process, a question came from the audience: "Do we even have a democracy?"

The way I answered at the time was to say there are degrees of democracy. American democracy is unquestionably in a weaker state and at greater risk than it has been at any time in living memory. But that is not to say it does not exist at all in our country. The fact that I could stand in a public place and harshly criticize my state government and condemn the social injustice inherent in today's politics and not be banned from campus or arrested is itself an indication of democracy's existence.

Days later, I found myself wishing I had answered differently. Not because I thought my answer was wrong. Just that I'd found a better one. It was staring up at me from a postcard sitting on my desk that had been sent to me by Ruth Meyer, the faithful assistant to Doris "Granny D" Haddock, after Granny's passing at the age of 100.

Granny D walked across America in an effort to dramatize the need to address growing political corruption by overhauling the way election campaigns are paid for. She was 90 years old when she completed her journey, reaching Washington, D.C. and circling Capitol Hill on foot until Congress passed the McCain-Feingold reform bill.

I met Doris for the first time when she was 93 at a forum on campaign financing held at the University of Wisconsin-Whitewater. We kept in touch after that, and I was able to persuade her to visit Wisconsin again to testify at the "public telling" we staged as part of our People's Legislature. She returned to my state several more times after that, most notably to speak at the annual Fighting Bob Fest.

On the card Ruth sent me is a photo of Doris standing on the steps of the New Hampshire Capitol with a quote at the bottom: *"Democracy is not something we have, it's something we do."*

Granny D was right about that. Democracy is more verb than noun. As long as we practice democracy, we have democracy. When we all stop acting as citizens in a democratic society, then and only then will democracy in America be truly dead.

We do democracy when we follow the money. We do democracy when we expose corruption in high places. We do democracy when we speak truth to power, and hold those in power accountable for their actions. We do democracy when we peaceably assemble and when we march and when we petition our government. We do democracy when we move to amend the constitution to reclaim meaningful free speech rights for the masses. We do democracy when we reject old labels and obsolete brands and dare to imagine a new political identity.

Change will come to American politics when enough of us believe something that most of us no longer do—that the power of the people is stronger than the people in power.

Too many of us have grown accepting of, or at least resigned to, money's dominion over politics. If there's to be a future for American democracy, we have to get over that. We have to become as intolerant of corrupt practices as the people of Wisconsin were at the turn of the twentieth century or even 40 years ago.

When enough of us cross that threshold and believe once again in the power of the people, endless possibilities will begin to present themselves to us.

It is possible to imagine someone running for office Bill Proxmire-style... with a modern twist. Instead of the Prox-for-our-age criss-crossing the land pressing the flesh all alone, it is possible to imagine a small army—maybe 50 or 100 in local or state legislative campaigns, 1,000 or 5,000 in a statewide contest, tens or even hundreds of thousands in national elections—taking to the sidewalks and the shopping mall parking lots and the country roads and becoming walking ads or living billboards to spread that Blue Jean candidate's message. Countless others could travel the electronic highways and byways of Facebook, Twitter and YouTube to do the same thing. People all across the country have started neighborhood book clubs. What is preventing us from establishing election clubs, where we would gather with friends and neighbors to share what we each know about the candidates, the offices they are seeking and the key issues in these races?

Instead of modern-day Proxes funding their campaigns with a few dollars from their own pockets, these crusades could be funded with a few dollars from a whole lot of pockets. It wouldn't be necessary to get half of the population or a quarter or even a tenth to start donating to such candidates in order to have a landscape-altering impact. *Five percent* would do. Just 5% of the population making small contributions of no more than $100 could collectively match or exceed the total amount given by the tiny segment of society giving vastly larger sums. A mere 5% of the population making modest political donations could free elected representatives from the clutches of the wealthy special interests that now control everything.

The point can be illustrated using national campaign contribution figures for 2009 and 2010. In that two-year election cycle, *one quarter of 1%* of Americans made political donations large enough to itemize; that is, big enough for federal law to require that the donors be identified. Those donors—a hair shy of 819,000 people out of the nation's estimated population of nearly 311 million—doled out just under $1.6 billion. That's an average donation of almost $2,000. Roughly the same amount of money would be generated if 5% of the 311 million, or about 15.5 million people, made contributions averaging $100.[1] Call it the "5% Solution."

Such a solution does not require the passage of any new law or reform of any existing system. It only requires legions of panhandlers for the politically homeless collecting enough small money to trump the big money and free us from the pay-to-say politics that has our government in a stranglehold. It can happen as soon as enough of us believe that the power of the people is stronger than the people in power.

We already have a tripartisan consensus—Republican, Democratic and independent voters alike—that money is playing far too great a role in our elections, is having a poisonous effect on governing, and needs to be reined in.

A recent Gallup Poll showed that half of Americans have reached the point of favoring banning campaign contributions altogether.[2] Even those who are best positioned to buy elections—namely America's top business leaders—are evidently getting tired of the political money game and have grown uncomfortable with elected officials being bought.[3] Three-quarters of them regard political giving as "pay to play" and close to 90% believe the campaign finance system needs to be overhauled.[4]

Seven in ten Americans believe the actions of elected officials reflect the values of the wealthy, not those of working-class people. Americans are united in their belief that money and lobbyists have too much influence in politics, with supermajorities of both Republicans and Democrats agreeing on this point. Eight in ten Americans believe there is too much money spent on election campaigns, with 83% of Republicans and 80% of Democrats agreeing with the following statement: *"There is too much money concentrated among a small number of groups and individuals spent on political campaigns in America, and strict limits should be placed on campaign spending and contributions."*[5]

What we do not have yet is broad public belief that citizens have the capacity to force change on the politicians and their parties. Supermajorities of people of every political stripe are sick and tired of the rigged political game and the crooked players. Yet those players, the elected representatives of the sick and tired, stubbornly resist reform and shamelessly cater to the small number of groups and individuals who supply them with their campaign money. In a country whose founders rebelled against taxation without representation, we now have elected officials giving their cash constituents representation without taxation. What do their voting constituents get? Sicker and more tired.

MIKE McCABE

It'll end when the tripartisan consensus that the system is sick turns into a tripartisan rebellion against those who spread the disease.

If there has ever been a time that screams out for political innovation, this is it. Creating a plausible alternative to today's politics involves risk, but so does invention of any kind. Light will appear one day at the end of the tunnel. But knowing that is small comfort when you're feeling around in the dark. History is scariest when it is being made.

Abolitionists ended slavery. There was no risk involved with that? No possibility of failure? Suffragists got women the right to vote. There was no resistance to that? New Dealers created Social Security and wiped out poverty among the aged. No risk there either? A Great Society took on segregation, passed the Civil Rights Act and Voting Rights Act, launched a war on poverty and established Medicare. All of these undertakings involved considerable risk. And for every advance there were multiple failed attempts to move America forward.

We are journeying into a great unknown. We face a crisis in our democracy never seen in living memory. We are in the fight of our lives.

Talk about your turning points.

Do we play it safe? Do we keep doing what we've been doing? Or do we take a leap of faith?

How we, how you, answer these questions will be known soon enough. For now, I know this much: If there's to be any hope for the common good in America, we need uncommon politics.

And I know this: If we do risk the leap, if we do discard the old habits and dare to imagine new ways of doing democracy, then a makeover of American politics is in the offing.

Notes

CHAPTER 1

1. U.S. Census population figures http://quickfacts.census.gov/qfd/states/55/55019.html

2. U.S. Department of Agriculture statistics http://www.nass.usda.gov/Statistics_by_State/Wisconsin/Publications/County_Estimates/milk_cows.pdf

3. "Total Personal Income and Per Capita Personal Income: Wisconsin Counties and Metropolitan Areas," U.S. Department of Commerce, Bureau of Economic Analysis, Regional Economic Accounts, April 2012 http://worknet.wisconsin.gov/worknet_info/downloads/PCPI/bea_rank_2010.pdf

4. State rankings of personal income per capita by the U.S. Census Bureau and U.S. Bureau of Economic Analysis http://www.census.gov/compendia/statab/2012/ranks/rank29.html

5. Farm Aid grew out of the July 1985 Live Aid Concert when Bob Dylan said on stage, "Wouldn't it be great if we did something for our own farmers right here in America?" Willie Nelson, Neil Young and John Mellencamp agreed that family farmers needed help and set out to plan a benefit concert for America. The first Farm Aid show was put together in six weeks and was held on September 22, 1985 in Champaign, Illinois before a crowd of 80,000 people. It raised over $9 million for America's family farmers. http://www.farmaid.org/site/?c=qlI5IhNVJsE&b=2723673

6. Video of Suder speaking at a Tea Party rally is posted on YouTube at https://www.youtube.com/watch?v=16Plvq4elFE

7. Article 23 of the Universal Declaration of Human Rights states: "1) Everyone has the right to work, to free choice of employment, to just and favourable conditions of work and to protection against unemployment; 2) Everyone, without any discrimination, has the right to equal pay for equal work; 3) Everyone who works has the right to just and favourable remuneration ensuring for himself and his family an existence worthy of human dignity, and supplemented, if necessary, by other means of social protection; 4) Everyone has the right to form and to join trade unions for the protection of his interests." To read the entire document, check out the United Nations website at http://www.un.org/en/documents/udhr/

8. Official results of the November 2, 2010 general election in Wisconsin http://gab.wi.gov/elections-voting/results/2010/fall-general

9. "Walker Contributions Above $1,000 – April 24, 2012 through May 21, 2012" published online in May 2012 by the Wisconsin Democracy Campaign at http://www.wisdc.org/pr052912.php

10. Ibid

11. Official results of the June 5, 2012 recall election in Wisconsin http://gab.wi.gov/elections-voting/results/2012/recall-election

12. "Business Giving to GOP, Dems Dwarfs Labor," Wisconsin Democracy Campaign, March 17, 2011 http://wisdc.org/pr031711.php

13. "Class War Chests," Wisconsin Democracy Campaign, January 2004 http://www.wisdc.org/classwarchestscover.html

14. Jason DeParle, Robert Gebeloff and Sabrina Tavernise, "Older, Suburban and Struggling, 'Near Poor' Startle the Census," The New York Times, November 18, 2011 http://www.nytimes.com/2011/11/19/us/census-measures-those-not-quite-in-poverty-but-struggling.html

15. "Wage Gap is Stuck," National Committee on Pay Equity, September 2013 http://www.pay-equity.org/

16. Sarah Bryner and Doug Weber, "Sex, Money and Politics," Center for Responsive Politics, September 26, 2013 http://www.opensecrets.org/news/reports/gender.php

17. Connie Cass, "Poll Reveals Americans Don't Trust Each Other Anymore," The Associated Press, November 30, 2013 http://www.huffingtonpost.com/2013/11/30/poll-americans-trust_n_4363884.html

18. Dave Gilson and Carolyn Perot, "It's the Inequality, Stupid," Mother Jones, March/April 2011 Issue http://www.motherjones.com/politics/2011/02/income-inequality-in-america-chart-graph

19. David Cay Johnston, Perfectly Legal: The Covert Campaign to Rig Our Tax System to Benefit the Super Rich – and Cheat Everybody Else, 2005

20. Craig Gilbert and John Schmid, "Wisconsin falls to 44th in private-sector job creation," Milwaukee Journal Sentinel, March 28, 2013 http://www.jsonline.com/news/wisconsin/wisconsin-private-sector-job-creation-ranking-declines-799bcsa-200435291.html

21. Mary Bottari, "Will Scott Walker Be Given a Pink Slip, an Orange Jump Suit or a Second Chance?" Center for Media and Democracy, June 3, 2003 http://www.prwatch.org/news/2012/06/11566/will-scott-walker-be-given-pink-slip-orange-jump-suit-or-second-chance

22. Craig Gilbert, "Scott Walker: Could he be the most polarizing governor in America?" Milwaukee Journal Sentinel, March 8, 2011 http://m.jsonline.com/top-stories/117577493.html

23. "Walker Post-Election Contributions Above $1,000" Wisconsin Democracy Campaign, July 6, 2012 http://www.wisdc.org/pr070612.php

MIKE McCABE

CHAPTER 2

1. The cover as well as the contents of the November/December 2011 edition of *Foreign Affairs* can be viewed online at http://www.foreignaffairs.com/issues/2011/90/6

2. George Packer, "The Broken Contract: Inequality and American Decline," *Foreign Affairs*, November/December 2011 http://www.foreignaffairs.com/articles/136402/george-packer/the-broken-contract

3. Emmanuel Saez, "Striking it Richer: The Evolution of Top Incomes in the United States" University of California, Berkeley Department of Economics, March 2, 2012, http://elsa.berkeley.edu/~saez/saez-UStopincomes-2010.pdf

4. John D. Buenker, Ph.D., "Progressivism Triumphant: The 1911 Wisconsin Legislature," feature article, Wisconsin Blue Book, 2011 http://legis.wisconsin.gov/lrb/bb/11bb/Feature.pdf

5. Erin Richards and Amy Hetzner, "Choice schools not outperforming MPS," *Milwaukee Journal Sentinel*, March 29, 2011 http://www.jsonline.com/news/education/118820339.html

6. Katie Ash, "Milwaukee Public Schools Outperform Voucher Schools in Program, Report Says," *Education Week*, February 13, 2013 http://blogs.edweek.org/edweek/charterschoice/2013/02/milwaukee_public_schools_outperforms_schools_in_voucher_program.html

7. Erin Richards and Patrick Simonaitis, "Most students applying for state voucher program attend private schools," *Milwaukee Journal Sentinel*, August 15, 2013 http://www.jsonline.com/news/education/most-students-applying-for-state-voucher-program-attend-private-schools-b9976473z1-219789131.html

8. The numbers cited here showing the disparity between political donations from pro-voucher interests and contributions from those opposed to school privatization were published on the Wisconsin Democracy Campaign's blog on September 23, 2013 with links to other reports and analyses. http://blog.wisdc.org/2013/09/influence-to-ninth-power.html

CHAPTER 3

1. A summary of the bill (HR 5005) and a list of its congressional cosponsors can be found on the Library of Congress website at http://thomas.loc.gov/cgi-bin/bdquery/z?d107:HR05005:@@@P

2. "Trends in Party Affiliation," Pew Research Center for the People and the Press, June 4, 2012 http://www.people-press.org/2012/06/04/section-9-trends-in-party-affiliation/

3. To dig deeper into what government spends on corporate subsidies compared to what is spent on the social safety net, see "Government Spends More on Corporate Welfare Subsidies than Social Welfare Programs" published online at http://thinkbynumbers.org/government-spending/corporate-welfare/corporate-welfare-statistics-vs-social-welfare-statistics/ and David Wildman's essay "Corporate Welfare Versus Social Welfare" at http://gbgm-umc.org/Response/articles/corporate_welfare.html.

4. Timothy Noah, "David Stockman: Working-Class Hero," Slate.com, September 4, 2003 http://www.slate.com/articles/news_and_politics/chatterbox/2003/09/david_stockman_workingclass_hero.html

5. "Serving the Have-Mores," Wisconsin Democracy Campaign, March 16, 2005 http://www.wisdc.org/sp031605.php

6. Job creation and unemployment trends in Wisconsin are aptly analyzed and visually depicted in *Wisconsin Job Watch*, a monthly publication of the University of Wisconsin-affiliated Center on Wisconsin Strategy that tracks Wisconsin's jobs deficit. http://www.cows.org/wisconsin-job-watch

7. "Serving the Have-Mores," Wisconsin Democracy Campaign, March 16, 2005 http://www.wisdc.org/sp031605.php

8. Legislative Audit Bureau report on the operations of the Wisconsin Economic Development Corporation, May 2013 http://legis.wisconsin.gov/lab/reports/13-7highlights.htm

9. "Who Pays? A Distributional Analysis of the Tax Systems in All 50 States," The Institute on Taxation and Economic Policy, January 2013 http://www.itep.org/whopays/

10. Jack Abramoff, *Capitol Punishment*, 2011

11. Learn more about the People's Legislature online at http://www.peopleslegislature.org/

12. Daniel P. Tokaji, "America's Top Model: The Wisconsin Government Accountability Board," Michael E. Moritz College of Law at The Ohio State University, January 16, 2013 http://papers.ssrn.com/sol3/papers.cfm?abstract_id=2201587

13. "High Court Race Cost Record $5.8 Million," Wisconsin Democracy Campaign, July 23, 2007 http://www.wisdc.org/pr072307a.php

14. More about Wisconsin's caucus scandal can be found online at http://www.wisdc.org/wdc_caucus_scandal.php. A compendium of news stories on the subject that appeared in the state's largest newspaper, the *Milwaukee Journal Sentinel*, can be found at http://www3.jsonline.com/news/state/caucus/index.asp

MIKE McCABE

15. Jeffrey M. Jones, "Congress' Approval Rating Remains Near Historical Lows," Gallup, August 13, 2013 http://www.gallup.com/poll/163964/congress-approval-rating-remains-near-historical-lows.aspx

CHAPTER 4

1. *Time* Magazine published an account of the tale end of Joe McCarthy's tenure as senator entitled "Wisconsin: Running Scared" on August 26, 1957. There also is an online compendium of resources about McCarthy's successor William Proxmire at http://en.wikipedia.org/wiki/William_Proxmire

2. Richard Severo, "William Proxmire, Maverick Democratic Senator From Wisconsin, Is Dead at 90,"*The New York Times*, December 16, 2005

3. One good profile of the career of Senator William Proxmire was published by the Wisconsin Historical Society and is available online at http://www.wisconsinhistory.org/topics/proxmire/biography.asp. An obituary written by The Associated Press after Proxmire's death also captures the essence of his political career. http://www.legacy.com/NS/Obituary.aspx?pid=15984365

4. "Recall Race for Governor Cost $81 Million," Wisconsin Democracy Campaign, July 25, 2012 http://www.wisdc.org/pr072512.php

5. Dee J. Hall, "State Employees Secretly Campaign," *Wisconsin State Journal*, May 20, 2001. This and other related news stories on the subject have been compiled and posted online by University of Wisconsin-Oshkosh professor Tony Palmeri at http://www.uwosh.edu/faculty_staff/palmeri/commentary/caucus.htm

6. Wisconsin Democracy Campaign, Caucus Scandal Archive, http://www.wisdc.org/wdc_caucus_scandal.php

7. "Before and After Citizens United: Wisconsin Election Spending Tripled in Wake of Supreme Court Ruling," Wisconsin Democracy Campaign, March 13, 2013 http://www.wisdc.org/pr031113.php

8. Dee J. Hall and Mary Spicuzza, "Prosecutor closes John Doe investigation into former Scott Walker aides," *Wisconsin State Journal*, March 2, 2013 http://host.madison.com/news/local/crime_and_courts/prosecutor-closes-john-doe-investigation-into-former-scott-walker-aides/article_5952999e-8283-11e2-b977-001a4bcf887a.html#ixzz2kkKNwkqB

9. Patrick Marley and Jason Stein, "Walker wins recall race over Barrett," *Milwaukee Journal Sentinel*, June 6, 2012 http://www.jsonline.com/news/statepolitics/guvrace06-ku5ld5b-157364555.html

10. Concurring opinion of Justice David Prosser in State of Wisconsin ex rel. Ismael R. Ozanne, Plaintiff-Respondent v. Jeff Fitzgerald, Scott Fitzgerald, Michael Ellis and Scott Suder, Defendants, Case No. 2011AP613-LV & 2011AP765-W, June 14, 2011 http://www.wicourts.gov/sc/opinion/DisplayDocument.html?content=html&seqNo=66078

11. Jason Stein, "Walker administration would charge Capitol protesters for police, cleanup," *Milwaukee Journal Sentinel*, December 1, 2011 http://www.jsonline.com/news/statepolitics/walker-administration-alters-protest-permit-requirements-6839brh-134845183.html

12. http://docs.legis.wisconsin.gov/constitution/wi/I/4

CHAPTER 5

1. "Class War Chests," Wisconsin Democracy Campaign, January 26, 2004 http://www.wisdc.org/pr012604.php

2. "Legislators Rely on Special Interests More Than Voters," Wisconsin Democracy Campaign, June 16, 2010 http://www.wisdc.org/pr061610.php

3. "Vermont and Rhode Island Had the Highest Percentages of Adults Contributing in 2010 and 2006 State Elections; New York, Utah, California and Florida the Lowest," Campaign Finance Institute research on state and local elections, December 20, 2012 http://www.cfinst.org/Press/PReleases/12-12-20/VT_and_RI_Had_the_Highest_Percentages_of_Adults_Contributing_in_2010_and_2006_State_Elections_NY_UT_CA_and_FL_the_Lowest.aspx

4. "Election Analysis: 2010 Midterm Bankrolled By Less Than 1% Of Americans Representing K Street, Wall Street Special Interests," Americans for Campaign Reform, January 26, 2011 http://www.acrreform.org/news/press/election-analysis-2010-midterm-bankrolled-by-less-than-1-of-americans-representing-k-street-wall-street-special-interests/

5. Center for Responsive Politics figures and analysis http://www.opensecrets.org/overview/donordemographics.php

6. Lee Drutman, "The Political 1% of the 1% in 2012," Sunlight Foundation, June 24, 2013 http://sunlightfoundation.com/blog/2013/06/24/1pct_of_the_1pct/

7. "Spreading Suppression: Restrictive Voting Laws Across the United States," Fair Elections Legal Network, August 7, 2012 http://www.fairelectionsnetwork.com/spreading-suppression-restrictive-voting-laws-across-united-states

8. John Schwartz, "Judge in Landmark Case Disavows Support for Voter ID," *The New York Times*, October 15, 2013 http://www.nytimes.com/2013/10/16/us/politics/judge-in-landmark-case-disavows-support-for-voter-id.html

9. Nick Wing, "Pennsylvania Voter ID Law Trial Set to Begin As State Concedes It Has No Proof," *The Huffington Post*, July 24, 2012 http://www.huffingtonpost.com/2012/07/24/pennsylvania-voter-id-trial_n_1697980.html

10. "Study: 500,000 Americans Could Face Significant Challenges to Obtain Photo ID to Vote," Brennan Center for Justice at New York University School of Law, July 18, 2012 http://www.brennancenter.org/press-release/study-500000-americans-could-face-significant-challenges-obtain-photo-id-to-vote

11. Richard L. Hasen, "Voter Suppression's New Pretext," *The New York Times*, November 15, 2013 http://www.nytimes.com/2013/11/16/opinion/voter-suppressions-new-pretext.html

12. Mark Binker, "Q&A: Changes to North Carolina Election Laws," WRAL-TV and WRAL.com, August 12, 2013 http://www.wral.com/election-changes-coming-in-2014-2016/12750290/

13. "Suppressing the Vote," The Daily Show with Jon Stewart, October 23, 2013 http://www.thedailyshow.com/watch/wed-october-23-2013/suppressing-the-vote

14. "Graft Tax," Wisconsin Democracy Campaign, January 13, 2003 http://www.wisdc.org/grafttax.php

15. David Callender, "Watchdog's bark gets louder, irks state legislators," *The Capital Times*, October 8, 2003

16. "Gagging Democracy," Wisconsin Democracy Campaign, August 4, 2005 http://www.wisdc.org/sp080405.php

17. Erik Kain, "Wisconsin Republicans Sneak Through Union-Busting Bill Without Democrats," *Forbes*, March 9, 2011 http://www.forbes.com/sites/erikkain/2011/03/09/wisconsin-republicans-sneak-through-union-busting-bill-without-democrats/

18. "Wisconsin ad says workers get pay taken away but major corporations get tax breaks," *Tampa Bay Times* and Politifact.com, March 4, 2011 http://www.politifact.com/truth-o-meter/statements/2011/mar/04/progressive-change-campaign-committee/wisconsin-ad-says-workers-get-pay-take-major-corpo/

19. "Special Interest Smorgasbord," Wisconsin Democracy Campaign, May 21, 2012 http://www.wisdc.org/sp052112.php

20. "Mine Backers Drill With Big Cash to Ease Regulations," Wisconsin Democracy Campaign, January 28, 2013 http://www.wisdc.org/pr012813.php

21. Dee J. Hall and Matthew DeFour, "Inner workings of influential pro-business group ALEC revealed," *Wisconsin State Journal*, December 5, 2013 http://host.madison.com/wsj/news/local/govt-and-politics/inner-workings-of-influential-pro-business-group-alec-revealed/article_f5168827-079c-5b33-b1df-89865be-46c2a.html

22. Roger D. Hodge, "Speak, Money," *Harper's*, October 2010 http://harpers.org/archive/2010/10/speak-money/

23. "The Rising American Electorate," Voter Participation Center http://www.voterparticipation.org/the-rising-american-electorate/

24. Hope Yen, "Census: White Majority in U.S. Gone by 2043," The Associated Press, June 13, 2013 http://usnews.nbcnews.com/_news/2013/06/13/18934111-census-white-majority-in-us-gone-by-2043

25. "Little Change in Public's Response to 'Capitalism,' 'Socialism,'" Pew Research Center for the People and the Press, December 28, 2011 http://www.people-press.org/2011/12/28/little-change-in-publics-response-to-capitalism-socialism/

26. John Light, "The Link Between Mass Incarceration and Voter Turnout," Moyers & Company, May 15, 2013 http://billmoyers.com/2013/05/15/the-link-between-mass-incarceration-and-voter-turnout/

27. "McCutcheon v. FEC," Brennan Center for Justice at New York University School of Law, April 2, 2014 http://www.brennancenter.org/legal-work/mccutcheon-v-fec

CHAPTER 6

1. Federalist No. 52 http://www.foundingfathers.info/federalistpapers/fed52.htm

2. Federalist No. 57 http://www.constitution.org/fed/federa57.htm

3. "Americans Bravely Go To Polls Despite Threat of Electing Congress," The Onion, November 2, 2010http://www.theonion.com/articles/americans-bravely-go-to-polls-despite-threat-of-el,18394/

4. One good source of information about proportional representation is FairVote, the national Center for Voting and Democracy. http://www.fairvote.org/fair-voting-proportional-representation

5. One of the more common forms of ranked-choice voting is a system called Instant Runoff Voting. The national group FairVote is a good place to go for more information. http://www.fairvote.org/instant-runoff-voting

6. "Top Contributors to Barack Obama," Center for Responsive Politics http://www.opensecrets.org/pres08/contrib.php?cycle=2008&cid=N00009638

7. Steven A. Holmes, "An Eccentric but No Joke; Perot's Strong Showing Raises Questions on What Might Have Been, and Might Be," The New York Times, November 5, 1992

8. "Former governor's brother Ed Thompson dies at 66," The Associated Press, October 22, 2011 http://host.madison.com/news/local/govt-and-politics/former-governor-s-brother-ed-thompson-dies-at/article_b40b572e-fcbd-11e0-8d98-001cc4c002e0.html

CHAPTER 7

1. John F. Kennedy, *Profiles in Courage*, 1957 http://www.goodreads.com/quotes/90682-if-by-a-liberal-they-mean-someone-who-looks-ahead

2. Jonathan Chait, "Paul Ryan: Poor People Need Jesus, Not Food," *New York Magazine*, November 19, 2013 http://nymag.com/daily/intelligencer/2013/11/paul-ryan-poor-people-need-jesus-not-food.html

3. Webster's definition of "conservative" is as good as any. http://www.merriam-webster.com/dictionary/conservative

4. Bruce Murphy, "How to Kill a Democracy," *Urban Milwaukee*, October 8, 2013 http://urbanmilwaukee.com/2013/10/08/murphys-law-how-to-kill-a-democracy/

5. Adam W. McCoy, "Glenn Grothman: Kwanzaa is Fake Holiday That 'Almost No Black People Today Care About,'" *The Huffington Post*, January 1, 2013 http://www.huffingtonpost.com/2013/01/01/glenn-grothman-kwanzaa_n_2392732.html

CHAPTER 8

1. The Wisconsin Historical Society has an extensive collection of materials about the birth of the Republican Party (http://www.wisconsinhistory.org/turningpoints/tp-022/?action=more_essay). Another source worth exploring is The Little White Schoolhouse, a nonprofit organization based in Oshkosh, Wisconsin (http://littlewhiteschoolhouse.com/).

2. "Petri right about GOP's future," *Wisconsin State Journal*, May 7, 2014 http://host.madison.com/wsj/news/opinion/editorial/petri-right-about-gop-s-future/article_c9bc6dee-bf3c-551d-9eda-daa7d8d52f05.html

3. "The Progressive Era: 1895 to 1925," Wisconsin Historical Society http://www.wisconsinhistory.org/topics/shorthistory/progressive.asp

4. Brendan DeMelle, "Study Confirms Tea Party by Big Tobacco and Billionaire Koch Brothers," *The Huffington Post*, February 11, 2013 http://www.huffingtonpost.com/brendan-demelle/study-confirms-tea-party-_b_2663125.html

5. Frank Rich, "The Billionaires Bankrolling the Tea Party," *The New York Times*, August 28, 2010 http://www.nytimes.com/2010/08/29/opinion/29rich.html

CHAPTER 9

1. "Early Colonial Comics," Fine Art Comics, March 17, 2013 http://fineart-comic.blogspot.com/2013/03/early-colonial-comics.html

2. Tamarine Cornelius, "Wisconsin's School Funding Cuts Among the Nation's Deepest," Wisconsin Budget Project, September 12, 2013 http://www.wisconsin-budgetproject.org/wisconsins-school-funding-cuts-among-the-nations-deepest-2

3. Mike Ivey, "Scott Walker's income tax cuts, by their very nature, skew toward wealthy," *The Capital Times*, February 21, 2013 http://host.madison.com/news/local/writers/mike_ivey/scott-walker-s-income-tax-cuts-by-their-very-nature/article_71e7a006-7c59-11e2-be42-0019bb2963f4.html

4. Lawrence R. Jacobs, "Right vs. Left in the Midwest," *The New York Times*, November 23, 2013 http://www.nytimes.com/2013/11/24/opinion/sunday/right-vs-left-in-the-midwest.html

CHAPTER 10

1. "Across the Aisle: The Growing Trans-partisan Opposition to Citizens United," report compiled by Free Speech for People, June 2013 http://freespeech-forpeople.org/sites/default/files/AcrossTheAisle-6-10-2013.pdf

2. The full opinion of the U.S. Supreme Court in *Santa Clara County v. Southern Pacific Railroad*, complete with the court reporter's notes, is available online at http://reclaimdemocracy.org/santa_clara_vs_southern_pacific/

3. "McCutcheon Money: The Projected Impact of Striking Aggregate Contribution Limits," Demos and U.S. PIRG, October 4, 2013 http://www.brennancenter.org/legal-work/mccutcheon-v-fec

4. There is no better source on the structure and activities of Super PACs than the Center for Responsive Politics. http://www.opensecrets.org/pacs/superpacs.php?cycle=2010

5. Adam Lioz and Blair Bowie, "Elected by 32 Donors, for 32 Donors," *The American Prospect*, January 17, 2013 http://prospect.org/article/elected-32-do-nors-32-donors

6. Thomas Jefferson letter to George Logan on November 12, 1816.

7. An excellent overview of this case and the Supreme Court's decision is provided by the Brennan Center for Justice at New York University School of Law. http://www.brennancenter.org/legal-work/federal-election-commission-v-wisconsin-right-life-inc

8. Jefferson letter of March 22, 1812 to François Adriaan van der Kemp.

CHAPTER 11

1. "Presidential Campaign TV AD Spending Expected to Surpass $1 Billion," The Associated Press, September 8, 2012 http://washington.cbslocal.com/2012/09/08/presidential-campaign-tv-ad-spending-expected-to-surpass-1-billion/

2. "Free Air Facts," Wisconsin Democracy Campaign, June 11, 2002 http://www.wisdc.org/free-air-facts.php

3. The source here is "Net Neutrality 101," a primer on the subject published on SaveTheInternet.com, a website sponsored by the national group Free Press. http://www.savetheinternet.com/net-neutrality-101

4. Richard R. Beeman, Ph.D., "Perspectives on the Constitution: A Republic, If You Can Keep It," National Constitution Center http://constitutioncenter.org/learn/educational-resources/historical-documents/perspectives-on-the-constitution-a-republic-if-you-can-keep-it

CHAPTER 12

1. Annie Lowrey, "The Rich Get Richer Through the Recovery," *The New York Times*, September 10, 2013 http://economix.blogs.nytimes.com/2013/09/10/the-rich-get-richer-through-the-recovery/

2. Kenneth Olmstead, Mark Jurkowitz, Amy Mitchell and Jodi Enda, "How Americans Get TV News at Home," Pew Research Journalism Project, October 11, 2013 http://www.journalism.org/2013/10/11/how-americans-get-tv-news-at-home/

3. Andrew Kohut, "Pew Research surveys of audience habits suggest perilous future for news," Pew Research Center, October 4, 2013 http://www.pewresearch.org/fact-tank/2013/10/04/pew-surveys-of-audience-habits-suggest-perilous-future-for-news/

4. John Mayer, lyrics to "Waiting on the World to Change" http://www.lyrics.com/waiting-on-the-world-to-change-lyrics-john-mayer.html

5. Michael Dolny, "We Paid $3 Billion for These Stations. We'll Decide What the News Is," Fairness and Accuracy in Reporting, June 1, 1998 http://fair.org/extra-online-articles/we-paid-3-billion-for-these-stations-well-decide-what-the-news-is/

6. Christine Y. Chen, "The Bad Boys of Radio Lowry Mays and sons made enemies building Clear Channel into an empire. Now they want to tell the world they're not..." *Fortune* Magazine, March 3, 2003 http://money.cnn.com/magazines/fortune/fortune_archive/2003/03/03/338343/

7. This statistic comes courtesy of the Media Reform Information Center, which cites Bagdikian's books among many other sources. http://www.corporations.org/media/

8. To learn more about the Franklin Center check out SourceWatch, the excellent online resource provided by the Center for Media and Democracy. http://www.sourcewatch.org/index.php?title=Franklin_Center_for_Government_and_Public_Integrity

9. To gain further insight into what the Sam Adams Alliance is and who is behind it, the Center for Media and Democracy's SourceWatch website is the place to start. http://www.sourcewatch.org/index.php/Sam_Adams_Alliance

10. Andy Kroll, "DonorsTrust – the Right's Dark-Money ATM – Pumps Out Record $96 Million," *Mother Jones*, December 3, 2013 http://www.motherjones.com/politics/2013/12/donors-trust-franklin-center-alec-mercatus-center-dark-money

11. "Election 2000 – Politicians and the Press: What are the dangers when journalism becomes entertainment and politicians become celebrities?" *Nieman Reports*, The Nieman Foundation for Journalism at Harvard University, Summer 2000 http://www.nieman.harvard.edu/assets/pdf/Nieman%20Reports/backissues/00summer.pdf

12. Gene Gibbons, "Ants at the Picnic: A Status Report on News Coverage of State Government," Joan Shorenstein Center on the Press, Politics and Public Policy, June 2010 http://shorensteincenter.org/wp-content/uploads/2012/03/d59_gibbons.pdf

13. Pew Center Project for Excellence in Journalism, Watchdog.org, *Assessing a New Landscape in Journalism*, organizational report, July 18, 2011

14. Dennis Chaptman, "Negative campaign ads contribute to a healthy democracy, political scientist argues," University of Wisconsin-Madison News, January 14, 2008 http://www.news.wisc.edu/14606

CHAPTER 13

1. Matt Rosenberg, "Gerrymandering: How States Create Congressional Districts Based on Census Data," About.com Geography http://geography.about.com/od/politicalgeography/a/gerrymandering.htm

2. "Sen. Mary Lazich: Redistricting should stay in hands of elected officials," *Wisconsin State Journal*, August 18, 2013 http://host.madison.com/wsj/print_only/columnist/sen-mary-lazich-redistricting-should-stay-in-hands-of-elected/article_6ddcf39d-2877-50a2-b6bd-29a0032c7136.html

3. Eric Ostermeier, "The Top 50 Most Competitive U.S. House Districts in the Nation," *Smart Politics*, Humphrey School of Public Affairs, University of Minnesota, March 16, 2010 http://blog.lib.umn.edu/cspg/smartpolitics/2010/03/the_top_50_most_competitive_us.php

4. "United States House of Representatives elections in Wisconsin, 2012" Ballotpedia.org http://ballotpedia.org/United_States_House_of_Representatives_elections_in_Wisconsin,_2012

5. "Redistricting battle cost taxpayers $2.1M," The Associated Press, November 2, 2013 http://www.channel3000.com/news/politics/redistricting-battle-cost-taxpayers-21m/-/4030/22774898/-/sjwxae/-/index.html

6. Nick Wing, "GOP REDMAP Memo Admits Gerrymandering To Thank For Congressional Election Success," *The Huffington Post*, January 17, 2013 http://www.huffingtonpost.com/2013/01/17/gop-redmap-memo-gerrymandering_n_2498913.html

CHAPTER 14

1. Jessica VanEgeren, "Bradley-Prosser incident reveals void in workplace safety rules for elected officials," *The Capital Times*, August 29, 2011 http://host.madison.com/ct/news/local/govt-and-politics/capitol-report/article_330b3daa-d22a-11e0-8aa1-001cc4c03286.html

2. Sandy Cullen and Gena Kittner, "Supreme Court members say Prosser a hot-head who has 'temper tantrums,' " *Wisconsin State Journal*, August 26, 2011 http://host.madison.com/wsj/news/local/crime_and_courts/article_cfa4cd18-d04d-11e0-aa9a-001cc4c03286.html

3. Dee J. Hall, "State Supreme Court dispute may be tough to decide," *Wisconsin State Journal*, September 11, 2011 http://host.madison.com/wsj/news/local/crime_and_courts/article_916d769a-dc77-11e0-85c7-001cc4c002e0.html

4. This passage is excerpted from a March 12, 2008 article entitled "Wisconsin Supreme Court among nation's most influential high courts," published by the Wisconsin Court System, citing the UC Davis Law Review study and a March 11, 2008 column by *New York Times* legal affairs correspondent Adam Liptak. http://www.wicourts.gov/news/view.jsp?id=69

5. "High Court Race Cost Record $5.8 Million," Wisconsin Democracy Campaign, July 23, 2007 http://www.wisdc.org/pr072307a.php

6. "Support Reveals Nonpartisan Farce of High Court Race," Wisconsin Democracy Campaign, March 13, 2007 http://www.wisdc.org/pr031307.php

7. Brian E. Clark, "Supreme Court ruling means state take $300 million tax hit," WisBusiness.com, July 11, 2008 http://wisbusiness.com/index.iml?Article=130783

8. "Nasty Supreme Court Race Cost Record $6 Million," Wisconsin Democracy Campaign, July 22, 2008 http://www.wisdc.org/pr072208.php

9. Patrick Marley, Steven Walters and Stacy Forster, "TV ad by Gableman comes out swinging," *Milwaukee Journal Sentinel*, March 15, 2008 http://www.jsonline.com/news/statepolitics/29486784.html

10. The reports cited here are an ongoing series entitled "The New Politics of Judicial Elections" published by the national court-reform group Justice at Stake. http://www.justiceatstake.org/resources/the-new-politics-of-judicial-elections/

11. The Brennan Center for Justice provides an excellent overview of this case and the court's ruling. http://www.brennancenter.org/legal-work/caperton-v-massey

12. "Judicial Recusal Reform: Two Years after Caperton," Brennan Center for Justice at New York University School of Law, June 2, 2011 http://www.brennancenter.org/analysis/judicial-recusal-reform-%E2%80%93-two-years-after-caperton

13. Greg Bump, "Prosser Vouches for Jensen's Character," WisPolitics.com, March 7, 2006 http://courtwatch.wispolitics.com/2006/03/prosser-vouches-for-jensens-character.html

14. Mike Johnson and Jason Stein, "Jensen settles misconduct case; felonies dropped," *Milwaukee Journal Sentinel*, December 20, 2010http://www.jsonline.com/news/waukesha/112195794.html

15. Jack Craver, "What constitutes illegal coordination in Wisconsin campaigns?" *The Capital Times*, December 2, 2013 http://host.madison.com/ct/news/local/writers/jack_craver/what-constitutes-illegal-coordination-in-wisconsin-campaigns/article_cc117a2c-57ad-11e3-8cfc-0019bb2963f4.html

16. "Southern Poverty Law Center: Hate Groups Numbers Up By 54% Since 2000," Reuters News Service, February 26, 2009 http://www.reuters.com/article/2009/02/26/idUS222404+26-Feb-2009+PRN20090226

17. Adam Skaggs and Andrew Silver, "Promoting Fair and Impartial Courts through Recusal Reform," Brennan Center for Justice, August 2011 http://www.brennancenter.org/publication/promoting-fair-and-impartial-courts-through-recusal-reform

18. One good source about "merit selection" of judges is the American Judicature Society. http://www.judicialselection.us/uploads/documents/ms_descrip_1185462202120.pdf. Also see Jona Goldschmidt, "Merit Selection: Current Status, Procedure and Issues," University of Miami Law Review, Fall 1994.

CHAPTER 15

1. Andrea Anderson, "Wisconsin and Madison above average in ACT test scores for 2013 graduates," *Wisconsin State Journal*, August 21, 2013 http://host.madison.com/news/local/wisconsin-and-madison-above-average-in-act-test-scores-for/article_2775d05e-799f-5a09-9476-2c4920d8438c.html

2. This famous Jefferson quote is found in an article on the Common School Movement taken from the Gale Encyclopedia of Education and published on Answers.com. http://www.answers.com/topic/common-school-movement

3. Ibid.

4. Ibid.

5. John Nichols, "State poised to renew progressive legacy this summer," *The Capital Times*, June 29, 2011 http://host.madison.com/ct/news/opinion/column/john_nichols/article_e80def6c-df6f-5646-9488-966ceca6d825.html

CHAPTER 16

1. "The Generation Gap and the 2012 Election: Angry Silents, Disengaged Millennials," Pew Research Center, November 3, 2011 http://www.people-press.org/files/legacy-pdf/11-3-11%20Generations%20Release.pdf

2. "Millennials: Confident. Connected. Open to Change." Pew Research Center, February 24, 2010 http://www.pewsocialtrends.org/2010/02/24/Millennials-confident-connected-open-to-change/

3. Peter Beinart, "Will Disillusioned Millennials Bring an End to the Reagan-Clinton Era?" Moyers & Company, September 12, 2013 http://billmoyers.com/2013/09/12/will-disillusioned-millennials-bring-an-end-to-the-reagan-clinton-era/

4. John Halpin and Karl Agne, "The Political Ideology of the Millennial Generation," Center for American Progress, May 2009 http://www.americanprogress.org/wp-content/uploads/issues/2009/05/pdf/political_ideology_youth.pdf

5. This is a second citation of the February 2010 Pew Research Center report, "Millennials: Confident. Connected. Open to Change." http://www.pewsocialtrends.org/2010/02/24/millennials-confident-connected-open-to-change/

6. David Madland and Amanda Logan, "The Progressive Generation: How Young Adults Think About The Economy," Center for American Progress, May 2008 http://www.americanprogress.org/issues/2008/05/pdf/progressive_generation.pdf

7. Bureau of Labor Statistics data http://www.bls.gov/cps/cpsaat01.htm

8. Heidi Shierholz, Natalie Sabadish and Nicholas Finio, "The Class of 2013: Young graduates still face dim job prospects," Economic Policy Institute briefing paper, April 10, 2013 http://www.epi.org/files/2013/Class-of-2013-graduates-job-prospects.pdf

9. Ibid.

10. Andrew Martin and Andrew W. Lehren, "Student Loans Weighing Down a Generation With Heavy Debt," *The New York Times*, May 12, 2012 http://www.nytimes.com/2012/05/13/business/student-loans-weighing-down-a-generation-with-heavy-debt.html

11. Shierholz, Sabadish and Finio, EPI briefing paper, April 10, 2013 http://www.epi.org/files/2013/Class-of-2013-graduates-job-prospects.pdf

CHAPTER 17

1. For a flavor of what Wisconsin Dells has to offer today and a glimpse into its past, check out the city's official website. http://www.wisconsin-dells-wi.com/

2. The dictionary definition of "dalles" is different than the meaning of the term referenced on the Wisconsin Dells promotional website. I'm sticking with the dictionary. http://dictionary.reference.com/browse/dalle

3. The Wisconsin Historical Society has more to offer on Kilbourntown. This just scratches the surface. http://www.wisconsinhistory.org/dictionary/index.asp?action=view&term_id=12295&term_type_id=2&term_type_text=Places&letter=K

4. "Legislative Scandal: Barstow vs. Bashford," Historic Madison, Inc. http://www.historicmadison.org/Madison%27s%20Past/Newsletter/scandal.html

5. Joseph A. Ranney, "Legislators for sale: The railroad scandal of 1856," Wisconsin Court System https://www.wicourts.gov/courts/history/article15.htm

6. This information is gleaned from an article about Pump Carpenter published by Historic Madison, Inc. http://www.historicmadison.org/Madison%27s%20Past/connectingwithourpast/pumpcarpenter.html

7. "Before and After Citizens United: Wisconsin Election Spending Tripled in Wake of Supreme Court Ruling," Wisconsin Democracy Campaign, March 13, 2013 http://www.wisdc.org/pr031113.php

8. "Table 3: Top Walker Contributors," from July 25, 2012 Wisconsin Democracy Campaign report http://www.wisdc.org/pr072512.php#tbl3

CHAPTER 18

1. Center for Responsive Politics data http://www.opensecrets.org/overview/DonorDemographics.php?Cycle=2010

2. Katie Glueck, "Half want government-funded campaigns," Politico.com, June 24, 2013 http://www.politico.com/story/2013/06/government-funded-campaigns-poll-93229.html

3. Kurt Walters, "Survey: Business Leaders Want Reform of Campaign Finance System," Public Campaign, July 25, 2013 http://www.publicampaign.org/blog/2013/07/25/survey-business-leaders-want-reform-campaign-finance-system

4. Julie Bykowicz, "Business Executives Call Political Giving 'Pay to Play,'" Bloomberg News, July 24, 2013 http://www.bloomberg.com/news/2013-07-24/business-executives-call-political-giving-pay-to-play-.html

5. Bob Cohn, "21 Charts That Explain American Values Today," *The Atlantic*, June 27, 2012 http://www.theatlantic.com/national/archive/2012/06/21-charts-that-explain-american-values-today/258990/

ABOUT THE AUTHOR

Mike McCabe brings a farming background and a professional lifetime of experience in politics, journalism, public sector management and nonprofit leadership to his work as executive director of the Wisconsin Democracy Campaign, a nonpartisan watchdog group that tracks the money in state politics, exposes government corruption and works for reforms that make people matter more than money in politics. Under Mike's leadership, the Democracy Campaign was recognized by the Wisconsin Freedom of Information Council and the Society of Professional Journalists as the "Citizen Openness Advocate of the Year" for 2012. Mike is one of Wisconsin's leading whistle blowers and is among the nation's best political money trackers. His efforts have attracted the attention of national news networks including ABC, CBS, CNN, Fox, NBC, MSNBC, NPR and Al-Jazeera English, as well as newspapers including *The New York Times, Washington Post, USA Today* and *Wall Street Journal*, and magazines such as *Time* and *New Yorker*. Among the many media organizations citing Mike's work or quoting him in their stories are national news services such as The Associated Press, Bloomberg News, McClatchy and Reuters, as well as online political news sites like Politico.com, Slate.com, and *Huffington Post*. A much sought-after public speaker, Mike has made more than 1,400 presentations to a wide range of audiences over the course of his career.